Bernadine Ziegler

His Ultimate Path

DORRANCE
PUBLISHING CO
EST. 1920
PITTSBURGH, PENNSYLVANIA 15238

Dorrance Publishing Co
585 Alpha Drive
Suite 103
Pittsburgh, PA 15238
Visit our website at *www.dorrancebookstore.com*

ISBN: 978-1-4809-3096-4
eISBN: 978-1-4809-3119-0

A Beautiful Sunset

by Mark Ziegler

A sunset is God's way of saying "good night" to this part of the world. "I have given you sunlight, pretty flowers to look upon, wheat fields to harvest and hay to bale for the food I will give each of you. I thank each of you for respecting the beautiful world in which I have given you. The moonlight which shines upon you is my brightest flashlight to guide you to work or home from grandma's house. I will continue to use my flashlight to guide you home from a hard night's work. All this I do because I love my children.

A DEATH WISH

WRITTEN BY BERNADINE ZIEGLER ON 6/17/15

This is a moment in my life I wish I could forget. I think about this all the time, it happened on a very cold day, ice and snow everywhere, in the year ninety-six. I have a new job but I do not drive so I had to ask my sister-in law to drive me, I should have been surprised because she was always very angry and this day she wasn't, she came to the house and I got into her car, I said the pleasantries for the morning to her and I wanted to tell her a safe way down from my road to the main road, my road is like a cliff hanger and so is almost all the roads around here. When they are covered with ice and snow, they become deadly, before I could tell her she said I already know of a way I just said okay if you are sure! I adjusted my seat put my seat belt on, and she proceeded down, my worst fear! the highest most hilly road in this town and I know it is covered with ice. The car got stuck about half way down, I can see the main road and at that moment I knew she was trying to kill me and she didn't care if she went too.

I should of known better because weeks before this she tried killing my older sister but I had no other choice for a ride, she tried pushing her weight against the car to help it jump off the cliff with both of us in it, it did finally move off the cliff but the car didn't tip while it fell off, it was like someone or something was holding it in mid-air but all I could do for some reason was watch her and wonder if she was in such deep emotional pain why didn't she just say something to one of us? When my sister-in law Gaby looked at me and said do you feel that? I said what!? when I looked at her face, I saw a light! It was brighter than any light bulb. But I said to her do I feel what Gaby? She just said that I knew, I knew what the light was from, I knew who the light was for, it was not for her, but I also thought I was going to die, all I could think is why? Gaby finally said are we going to die? I realized then she really wanted to die but why take me, I thought, I did not long ago I made a promise to God that I wouldn't take my life again and now she is trying to finish the job. I saw the light separate and the second light went to the other side of the falling car on my side of the car I saw their faces of light there are two of them one on each side I wanted to ask Gaby if she saw them but she has been in like a frozen state for a while now, I just kept looking at them as they looked at me and smiled so bright. I knew then I was going to be okay whether I lived or died I was going to be okay.

The car was finally coming down. I knew this because the two angels shifted their heads so they weren't smiling at me anymore and their very long, large wing mass opened up to brace the car so they could place the car on its wheels gently so no harm would come to the both of us. The angels left after the car was placed safely on it wheels, the car was placed in front of a business just like we parked it there, I got out of the car on my side closed the door hard, Gaby also got out and then I said I am walking home. She is still frozen in thought even though she was also out of the car, I must admit I didn't check if she was alright I just didn't look back I didn't care what happened to her I just left her with the car, even though it could of exploded but for some reason I didn't care about her anymore, I know this is wrong but I guess I was frozen in thought also.

I continued to walk home, it took me a while because I am very cold and the roads are still covered, the city doesn't believe in cleaning the roads, but when I finally got to the house with no other incidents I open the door my mother was there, she was shocked to see me, she shouted why are you here!? I thought Gaby drove you to work! I just said quite angrily out loud Gaby tried killing me by driving off a cold icy cliff! Mom knew which one, I grabbed the phone started dialing my job and told them I was just in a car accident and that I wasn't coming in. They asked are you alright I said yes! But shaken up some I hung up the phone mom asked harshly where's Gaby!? I said I don't care I left her with the car she is alive and standing outside of the car.

Somehow I got a safe ride to my work even though I called off but I went to work anyway, everyone was shocked I showed up but I just had to get away from my house and the area, I will never forget my two angels God sent to protect me but I still wondered why not her because she is a bipolar, these people never realize their wrongs I did forgive her but even to this day I can't forget but I also think about her often wondering if things could have been a little different with my sister-in law. Let's just say I never went with her anywhere and I never asked her for anything ever again, but all she ever said was some day you will laugh about it, That is how a bipolar apologizes, well she is dead now from cancer, it has been five years since her death but I am still not laughing, but I still can't stop thinking why, why wouldn't she just talk to us why did she have to be like this and why did she choose to leave this world the way she did?

LETTER OF GOD'S LAWS

BY BERNADINE ZIEGLER (3-10-13)

God and I were wondering how His World is getting so messed up, when will all of you ever understand that God is Law? He made all the laws as we know them today. Does anyone remember Moses? How about the Ten Commandments?

The Burning Tree oh, how we need Thee. When will you understand that God is responsible for everything we walk on?

Everything time we breathe: just look around, don't make a sound, just listen you will Hear Him, Without Him: what or where would you be? The answer is nowhere and nothing! Trust me.

What makes you think that you have any right to take Him out of your life, what makes you think your life is your life? It's not, it's God's and yes! He gave us choice to be His Voice not your own, to stand as one in His Everlasting Love and Name, as for the government which He is responsible for, why you ask?

Let's try the Original Laws given to Moses, one fine day on Mount Sinai. So I ask why are you evil doers even in politics, who gives you the right to cause all of this destruction? When will it end?

Why are you trying to throw Him out the door? You have no right to do that; He has MORE than the right to throw you through the sky floor, and so much more. You have no idea. I do have one question; do you want to find this out the hard way? I would say no way! If you would like to, then all you have to do is keep it up. Don't worry, God will not only find you, He will also plague you, so watch what you do because the Great I Am He is known as will find you.

A PERFECT WORLD

⌒⌒

BY BERNADINE ZIEGLER
(7-13-10)

What is a perfect world anyway? Dogs, dogs, everywhere dogs, if we didn't have dogs in our world then where would we be? Who would be our constant barking alarm to protect and warn us of harm? Dogs will always be a part of my perfect world. Oh! How I miss my dogs, and wolves.

Cats, cats, everywhere cats, what would our world be like if there were no cats? Well just remember this, if there were no cats of all kinds, then we would be over ran by rodents of all sorts, cats will also remain in my perfect world for this and many other reasons.

Birds, birds, everywhere there are birds, what good are they in a perfect world? Well, for one they just don't have the beauty of flight both day and the night, there are many reasons why such as keeping the worm, bug, and snake populations down. They also give a reason for the trees and flowers to be around, oh! There wonderful song sounds.

What is a perfect world? Where is this perfect world? These are all good questions! There is so much to mention but it all boils down to one entity: His Name is God, The Perfect World is His World; the one He Created which is all the living and breathing things in this world are His, He is my everything, His Perfect World is my perfect world and always will be.

A PRAYER TO GOD

BY BERNADINE ZIEGLER
(3-5-13)

Forgive me Lord, I am a sinner. I beg for mercy, I'm sorry I've not done better. Bless me, and keep me Lord, teach me how to be one of your apostles, a Vessel of your Holy Word.

Have pity on me, I pray I never disappoint thee, please Dear Lord God, Don't leave me. Always keep me warm with Your Holy Light, keep me in your Loving Arms, and please hold me tight.

Please God don't deny me. I love thee; please keep me at your side, with your Guidance and Grace. Shield me from evils lure, Lord God; know I only answer to you.

Lord, I only obey you, you have my everlasting devotion, without Your Love, I wouldn't know what to do, my life would be nothing without you, life will never be the same, His Everlasting Love is His Name and Peace is His Everlasting Reign.

A WEDDING POEM

BY BERNADINE MISURA

(10-19-06)

Soon I will be able to call you my husband, my lover, by God's Will there will be no other, you are my gift from God, my love and devotion for you will always grow and grow. You are my best friend. Our marriage for God and to each other will never have an end. Soon I will say I do to you, and when this becomes true, we become one. Know I will always stand by you no matter what you or we go through. When we do have a fight and WE WILL. Before we go to our marriage bed we will make amends, we can then really mean I love you, and I wish you good night.

On that wonderful day I take you as my husband and I as your wife, we will become partners in life, and we will share God's Holy Light, no matter the problems and stress, I make you this forever promise, You are my heart, you are my soul, my love I give to you is and always will be as Pure as God's White Dove, even when we are not together, we will still be able to fight all of the unholy weather, because you are in my heart to never part, this I can promise to you.

BOOKS

BY BERNADINE MISURA
(7-21-06)

Books, books, everywhere there are books; I love them for so many reasons, no! Not just for their looks, they are not just a wealth of information, some you won't even hear from your news station, there are some that even discuss people's life situations or frustrations; there are some on even the constitution, if you can believe it even on resolutions. How do I ever decide what book to keep, buy, or deny.

There are so many books from the past, present and yes! Even the future, books have so many uses that people forget such as they can take you back in time, no! I don't mind! So how I find myself inclined to read a book for just the fantasy, or theology, to mythology, wow! Could there really be these kinds of books? I would have the best time.

They are not just a source of information, you can find one about almost anything such as: fish, hooks, these books are not just for looks, how about subjects in the news, such as politics, if you don't read about the world today in any kind of way, or what people will say you will defiantly lose, you can find out everyone's views, be careful not to snooze. Oh! The history, and the mystery, what a good buy this would be!

You can find a lot on religion, any kind or situation, reading about this subject you just can't miss, you will know your fate, and be able to decide your faith, for this I would not wait so go read a book; it doesn't hurt to take a look, at least take the chance on even sex, romance or how to perform in the dance, but don't forget to read the Good Book on all your vacations, no matter your station.

COME ALL

WRITTEN BY BERNADINE MISURA
ON 9-24-06

Come all ye angels, come all ye saints, come all who believe and love the Lord God in His Holy Place, who receives His Holy Grace. Come all ye sinners, and pray with all of us, we will pray for forgiveness, for you too. When you do believe in all of him and all the things, he does for you. You can feel His Holy Light, and your life will become anew.

God sacrificed his only son because of Adam, Eve, and all our original sin, let's stand and pray together so he doesn't have to do this again, don't you all understand that he loves us just that much, so I ask you why can't you all love him, just as much.

For all that would rather moan and complain, for those who kill, maim, and torture, to you I implore please, no more! On God's innocent little critters and creatures, for this your sins will remain. Amen, I say to you it's not to late to come to Jesus, to make a clean slate, by saying you're sorry! This will renew your faith, and decide your fate.

For those of you who just seem to not care about God's Scriptures, God's Grace, or even Jesus, on His Holy Cross, you maybe still think you will be still going to heaven, and being able to see his Holy Face, believe me you're in for a great fall.

The Angels, will say we can't do anything for you at all but say to hell is the only place for you.

Amen I say come all ye angels, come ye sinners, come all ye saints, let's stand together and say I love you, I adore you, I glorify you, I will always preserve you in my heart, I pray that we will never part. Come Holy Ghost, please heal us all with your Holy Host, lets all be as one for Jesus, God, and the Blessed Trinity.

God's Frozen Tears

By Mark Edward Ziegler
2/15/15

God watched in horror as the destruction of His beautiful world unfolded before His Eyes. God's frozen tears came from the skies.

Why must we give Him such a frown? When His Eternal Love was handed down? His Eternal Love was given to all to enjoy, When all we want to do is destroy.
A slap in the face to Him we gave, a path to hell did we pave.

We should ask for His forgiveness, YES, we should, before Him we all stood. Can we fix this, I don't know!

We must NOT make The Good Lord cry, Or we will surely die from his Frozen Tears known as snow.

DAY OF THE M.R.I.

BY BERNADINE ZIEGLER
(6/17/15)

I was on a cruise to Disney World, when I got on the ship I knew something felt odd. But different in a good way the cruise was after the twin towers came down and everywhere bombs but we the family went and enjoyed ourselves but what did I keep feeling I know I had a doctor's appointment as soon as I got off the ship but could that be it then I heard a voice, His Voice, God's Voice! He was telling me that I have been cured the test that I am to have tomorrow will find nothing for your epilepsy, I didn't want to not believe it but I couldn't tell anyone either, so I went to dinner on the cruise ship like nothing ever happened, but I know it did I couldn't be happy because I could not tell anyone they would need proof first, so I enjoyed the cruise without any signs that something is different for a whole wonderful week.

I returned home I almost went right to bed because I have an early morning doctor appointment, I was very nervous because I have never had a M.R.I. just a lot of E.E.G's, I just couldn't get God's message out of my head could it be true am I cured of the epilepsy that I have had since I can remember as I was growing up could this be real? They took me to the back and prepped me for this huge clear tube which I have never seen before in my whole life, I was getting real scared, they pulled out part of the tube I am supposed to lay on so I did as they told me, I laid down as still as possible the bed is so small as they slid the tube closed they kept talking to me telling me to not move and asking me questions such as what music I like to listen to I found out to calm me down so I told them the eighties, Billy Joel came on I think it was up town girl, I have never been confined like this so I felt like I was going to panic but somehow I stayed calm and didn't move an inch or hand.

A female came on and asked if I was okay, after some time I said yes! For now she said if you go to sleep it will be easier on me but I could never fall asleep during these medical tests, I just said no I am okay, some time went by it seemed like a long time I just want to lift my hand and bang on the tube window I also wanted to scream so bad but before I could even mutter a word which no one would hear anyway I saw two very large images in front of the white wall that was also in front of my face and the male image said loud and sternly don't move he put his hand out like you would to stop a car, the large female image said also don't move be still then the male said it is almost over be still or you will have to do this over, we need you to finish this we need you to get this done I must admit those last words did shock me, but I just couldn't take my eyes off them I think the medic asked if I was okay but I didn't answer at first I also heard her mutter is she asleep or alive, then I heard the female medic again ask if I was alright I finally said yes!

Then I looked to see if my angels were gone and to my joy they were still there in fact it was like they read my mind because the female angel said we will be here with you until it's over! I just couldn't take my eyes off of their wing mass they both had the largest wing mass I could possibly imagine on an angel the male opened his first it seemed like it spread out to the entire wall length and he even had two sets of wings and then I asked the question through my thoughts could I see yours she open hers and they were almost as large as his but I don't think she had two sets but they were long but when she opened hers there appeared a smaller angel like a cherub then she closed her wings but not all the way she wanted me to see the small one and then she said you are almost finished then the large male angel closed his wings slowly then he whispered you are almost finished be still don't move the three angels remained until the medics got me out of the tube it was the most awesome site I have ever seen, I hear the female medic say are you alright in there I said yes! I am fine but I was still watching my angels, then the medics came in the room but before they opened the tube my three angels left me the medics told me I did fine and when I would have the results of the test I think it was a couple of weeks but I just wanted to see my angels again but before they left me I used my thoughts to tell them thank you.

I am cured from epilepsy I have been for fourteen years now the test came back with no evidence of any epilepsy ever being there just an infected sinus tube on my left side, but I will never forget my three angels God had sent to me to keep me calm.

DEER'S CRY WHY?

BY BERNADINE MISURA

Deer's cry! why do you run over us? Is it just because
you are careless and when we get hit you humans
complain that you are careless and you can't go
anywhere? What about us, we will never be able to
roam to our home, why? Do you force us to say
goodbye to our loved ones? This you can't deny.

Deer's cry why? Don't you just slow down and let
us just get across before you go by? I bet you don't
even try, we have seen you just fly by, I just ask you
Why?

We don't want for much, just to go somewhere for
some lunch to munch, is that too much to ask? I beg
of you just let us pass. By slowing down because
you're coming towards us much too fast.

Why? Can't you watch for us and all of God's wild
Critters, we don't make a fuss so why do you hit us?
Is it just... Oh! We are in your way!

Or is it because you hate us for being here on the
same planet as you each and every day, is that why
you are making our food supply go away!

What did we ever do to you? There is
Nothing we can do or say, we just want to frolic and
play. We are deer we don't know how to brighten

your day! So please go another direction, just go away! So God's wild critters can laugh and play and live for another day. Okay?

DEPRESSION MOUNTAIN

⌒⌒

BY BERNADINE MISURA
(3/19/00)

My name is Johnathon Beardsley, I am ten years old, and I want to tell you a very unusual story. I live on Indian Cove in Serenity County in Montana, on a reservation called Trinity Hills, in the year 1736. I live with my mother her name is Sara. My dad was killed by a wild cat but I didn't get to see it. Anyway, one day my friend and I went out to play it was chilly but normal weather to us, my friends name is Josh Clearwater, and he is a native of this land just like my father. On the day I went out to play I asked my mom if I could go before dinner and chores, she said, "Okay, but not to go too far." I told her I am going to play with Josh Clearwater she said that would be fine if his mother is okay with it.

I must admit I was a little shocked because Josh is older than me but only by three years, I went to his house and then Josh took me to the mountain to where I was always told by my father to stay away from it but he never told me why? I must admit I was always curious why, but for some reason it also scared me to go there, Josh was showing me around the outside of the mountain he even told me there is a church buried somewhere within the Mountain, but it was getting a little dark and the lighting around the mountain is not very good, but from what my young eyes can see it is very large and to me a bit scary. Josh told me there is always a light that stays lit inside of the mountains cave. He went on to say there is also a lady that stays there, he said I think she lives in there and I said to him no way Josh you are just making up a story he kept trying to convince me that he was telling me the truth and that he has even gone into the cave and seen her and that she spoke to him.

At this point I just wasn't sure if he was telling me the truth but why would he lie to me I have asked him nothing so far. I did finally ask him is the mountain called Depression Mountain because of the lady inside? He said,

"You know I'm not really sure I just know what my father told to me." I asked Josh why don't you go in the cave now to see the lady? He took some quiet time before answering me and said she calls for another she calls for someone else then he stared at me with still strong burning blue eyes upon me. I was shocked I said I cannot go in there, I am only ten and I am not to be this far from home as it is and if we don't leave now my mother is going to throw a fit and then she will ban me from you. Josh said that is true but Josh also said I didn't mean today you have to be ready to see her to listen to what she has to tell you.

On our walk home all I could think about is what Josh told to me, Josh was still talking to me as we walked, but I wasn't listening to his words then we stopped and he shouted a few times at me while calling out my name. Jonathon! He shouted with anger and loudly he said what is the matter, what are you thinking about? Jonathon went on to ask is it what you told me at the mountain why is she calling for me? Who is she, why me, what does she want of me, my questions went unanswered but Josh did say if you can get away from your chores tomorrow we can go earlier in the day and maybe then you will be ready for the lady in the cave. Josh advised me to get some sleep and think this over and to not tell anybody especially your mother, I said I can't lie to my mother not telling her is the same thing, Josh said, "you must, you must not tell her about this she would not understand." We continued to walk home and I asked, is the lady beautiful? Josh said, "More beautiful than you can imagine."

As I was about to go into my house Josh said, "remember what I told you", I nodded my head in acknowledgement, I whispered I know, then I went into my house for supper, while Josh left for home, but I still couldn't not get any of this off my mind I feel scared and confused at the same time. I sat down at the table mother gave me dinner but I just couldn't seem to eat she noticed there is something on my mind. Mother asked me if I had a good time with Josh Clearwater, I looked up and say yes! Like I was confused at what she asked, she asked what is the matter? I whispered I can't speak about it mother Josh said you wouldn't understand. She looked at me kind of somberly and said, "Try me, I know, I know my boy."

I asked mom in a whisper mother can I be let out of my chores tomorrow Josh wants me to go with him early, like right after school, she held my chin in her hand and said okay but don't be too late I have to talk to you about your father, I thought it to be odd, so I just said yes Mother! I promise I'll be home before night fall, mom said hurry with your meal and then get ready for bed you have school in the morning. The next morning came I went to school and there I saw Josh, and I told him mother said I can go with you then I asked did your mother say it was okay for you? He just whispered she lets me go all the time since my father died, I was shocked I asked him when did he die? He said a few months ago a wild cat killed him I said my father died also a few months ago by a wild cat, I asked Josh what does that mean he answered I don't know, but that is odd. I thought to myself I will ask my mother when I get home she did say she has to tell me something about father anyway. I did my best to put that out of my mind for the day, so I can learn more at school.

The school day ended and Josh met up with me and he asked me if I was ready to go and motioned my head to say yes! He said, "Let's go!", so we went walking to the mountain, I asked him, why is it called Depression Mountain? He said my father told me the elders say it is because there is a weak point somewhere in the mountains floor if it is found and stepped upon it will fall through and so will everything else. I said oh! I thought it was called that for another reason, Josh asked what? I said, "I thought you were going to tell me that when people go there they hear a spirit of some kind always crying." Josh stopped and paused and said, "I originally thought that also, but no just because of a weakness in the rock."

We continued our journey to the mountain, because we are young it didn't take us long to get there but before we did I asked Josh more questions about the lady in the cave he proceeded in telling me that she always wears black like a nun in a church and that there is always a small fire burning in the middle of the cave I am not sure why, but it never goes out. Josh also said if you want to know more you must go into the cave and talk to the lady, I can't tell you anymore. josh said, "Okay I believe you Josh, but I still don't know why she wants me."

When we arrived we stopped just before the opening of the cave, I looked around at all the surroundings, and I could see even the inside. Josh was right. I saw the fire in the middle burning but a nice gentle fire no high flames, Josh was trying to push me in but I held onto the outer walls I said no not right now but I kept looking in the lady came near me and said my name and with words and with her hand motion she said come on in, I wanted to say no so bad but something stopped me from saying anything and I went in very slowly and Josh sat down on a nearby rock by the entrance way, I wanted so bad to run out of here but my feet just wouldn't move that way so I just kept looking around the cave, it is very large and there are a lot of writings and drawings all over the cave, I think the lady is adding them on the wall as the days go by, the lady came closer to me to where I can hear her she asked, "you noticed my writings on the wall?" she said, "my name is Paula", she looked down at her clothes she said, "I am a nun", then she asked me is your name Jonathan, are you the boy I am waiting for? I finally said something, I said, "I don't know why me, why are you here?"

But, all I could think of as I looked at her is that she is glowing with some light all around her. She is radiant there is something about her. Josh is right; she is very beautiful beyond my belief. Her smile is truly amazing to me. I couldn't stop looking at her. Is this wrong, why is this? I almost forgot about the promise I made to my mother, I said pretty lady then she said Paula, then I said Sister, I must go I made a promise to my mother, I came running out of the cave shouting for Josh, he didn't hear me at first, then I shouted again. I said we have to go it's almost night fall and I promised mother I wouldn't be home late. So we hurried home because he made the same promise and Josh said we are going to be in such trouble. I finally got home I ran inside mother said, "You are almost late." I said, "Yes mom I am sorry", she smiled and said, "Well you're home now, forget it," I admit that I am relieved to hear that.

Mother said hurry get washed up for supper and then I will tell you about your father, I washed and ate my dinner so fast, I think it was because I was going to get some answers to questions I may not have yet. And maybe some answers to the questions I have now, but most of all I get to learn more about father, I got my bed clothes on sat on my bed waiting for mother I called to her, mother, please tell me a story about father, she answered I am coming my son, she arrived not more than two minutes but it seemed longer she sat on my bed and smiled at me, caressed my face and said, "I'm not sure how to start so I ask first what did you discover today?" I said I saw a beautiful lady in a cave at Depression Mountain, I said her name is Paula, as in Sister Paula, mother just muttered, "Oh!"

Mother said that her real name is Sara Beardsley, I am French English descent but yours is not Beardsley, your last name is Clearwater just like Joshua's, your father's name is River Flows Clearwater, I am your fathers second wife Josh's mother is his first I know you know her as Cynthia Clearwater but her real name is Flows Swiftly Clearwater, it was your father's idea to change her name and your last name, Cynthia is now married to Soft Shoe, I said with shock, Chief Soft Shoe? Mother said yes! Your father arranged the marriage to protect us and Josh, so we can all stay on the reservation without malice.

Mother looked at me and asked me if I understand I whispered I think so, so she went on to say Jonathan if you haven't figured it out yet Josh is your brother, he is your father's son as you are he changed your name to Beardsley, so there would be no fights among the brothers for his love and because of his position, I said I don't understand mother she said I figured she went on to say your father was the chief of this nation and he did die because of a wild cat, it got into the tribe land it was large enough to kill the children. Your father loves all children as his but he loves you and Josh more and that is why he put himself in dangers way as the chief that is what you are supposed to do, then she whispered with tears in her voice I miss him terribly, then she looked at me and said please don't be angry with us, He told me tell you everything when you were ready I just never thought it would be this early. Mother asked me again do I understand I asked again Josh is my brother she said yes! With a smile then she asked didn't you wonder why I let you go with a bigger boy? I laughed and said I did but I'm ten years old mother, she caressed my face again and said yes you are. *I did how ever ask her does Josh know about any of this she said no not yet but I did have a talk with his mother while you were out with Josh, and she is going to tell him the truth.*

Mother asked me do you have any questions for now I said no! Okay then I will go on. The lady in the cave your father told me about her also and Depression Mountain, the lady is a messenger of God! And he knew that both of his sons were going to be called by Him that is why he arranged the marriage with Cynthia and Soft Shoe, so the tribe will be taken care of while his son's go and answer God's call. So now that you know you go when she calls you, you go with Josh but always be home by night fall that is all I ask of you. Then she looked into my eyes, would you please tell me what she asks of you? I want to know everything you and Josh go through but please don't get into anything that will cause you or Josh harm. I whispered I will mother and thanks, she kissed me and said the lady is a guide but I am also a guide to help you okay! Now you must get some sleep I know its Saturday tomorrow but the Lord still wants you to rest. I said yes! And good night.

Saturday finally arrived and I woke up as soon as the cock crowed, mother was already placing breakfast on the table. Josh came to the door; mother answered by saying Jonathan is having breakfast come on in Josh he said no, I will wait out here. Mother said to him he won't be long and I wasn't I hurried but mother said don't be late you have church in the morning, I said yes! Mother I promise. I heard her say go with God, my son!

I went outside Josh looked so emotional I knew what that meant but I still had to ask I said Josh do you know? He hugged me tightly and said yes! My brother I know then we walked on to the mountain. When we finally arrived at the mountain I looked around the outside of it and I never realized how amazing it looks and how beautiful the church looks and how easy it is to find in the light of day, when I went in this time I wasn't afraid, the sister was there asking me to come in I asked her by calling her Sister Paula, when did you live and die if I am allowed to ask she smiled and said you may! She said, "I was born in the year of our Lord 347 and died in the year of our Lord 404 and I was placed in this cave after my death," since Josh stayed outside again I have to ask all the questions I asked the sister since you died that long ago that makes you a Saint she said yes! I hear a man's voice off in the distance but it kind of sounds near I looked around and couldn't find it, it kept calling my name Jonathan Clearwater, the sister was showing me the pattern of the drawings on the wall and how I have to use them to open the wall to find His Voice, I thought to myself who is the voice, then I remembered what my mother said about church, then I saw the man on the cross.

I did as the sister told me and the wall opened up, I suddenly got frightened again, but I kept hearing my name Jonathan, come but the light is so bright, she said don't be scared, He will guide you as I have, now your will is to go to Him now He calls to you, Sister Paula said just follow the wall don't look into the light I said I can't see now but I started walking slowly to the male voice, He kept calling me so I knew which way to go as I was getting closer to the voice the light got even brighter, He said Jonathan close your eyes you don't need them in here, just listen to me I called upon you because of your father offered up his two sons to me for the purpose that I ask of you now, I said Lord I hear you, I am here for you, tell me, The Lord said I need you to become a priest when you are a little older but for now I need you and your companion your brother to spread my message of Innocence to all of the children of the nation to your tribe as well you must start with the children, then in time the elders will listen you need to show all my lost souls the way back home to me, what do you say Jonathan will you help me? I said I am here for you Lord and no other, my servant will guide you she will remain here for you.

The wall opened up and I slowly walked out to where Josh is. Josh seems very happy to see me, he said it has been four hours since you went in, I thought the wall ate you up. I had no idea of time, then I finally said to him, "Josh it is your turn the Lord calls you now He will open the wall for you, you must go into the cave and seek out Sister Paula," Josh seemed to hesitate for some reason. Then Josh said, "Since it is for God, I will go back in with you." he said, "alright I'll go." Then we went into the cave where Sister Paula motioned for Josh and then showed him the same way she showed me. The wall opened up Josh hesitated again, I said, "It's okay Josh, He loves you just follow the Voice in the wall then you will be fine, just don't look into the light just listen to Him and listen well I'll be here waiting for you," then he disappeared into the wall, I went outside to wait as Josh did for me, it did really take four hours as Josh said, Josh came out to me and told me the same stuff as the Lord said to me we are both going to be priests as we get older but as children we are to save the children from evil, and teach them to keep their Innocence, as God always commands.

We went back several times to speak to God or Sister Paula, to get answers sometimes we even went separately as we got older, but we couldn't be happier to the fact that we are not just brothers in Christ we are Brothers of the Clearwater, we both also kept our mothers informed by everything we do because as they both promised they will always be our guides, my brother and I have gone on many journeys some together some alone but in our hearts never far from home we are both priests now we haven't been back to Depression Mountain for a while but I did hear from Father Joshua, that he plans on opening a church and monastery on the reservation, and call it St. Paula, he said that he checks on our mothers often mine does write me, I long to see her and to tell her about my days I will be finishing up my first four years of being a priest and maybe by God's Will Father Joshua, will have the church open and he will call upon me to reside there with him, but I hear from him often but still I can't help but wonder if he has been there or has he seen The Lady in the cave I can't help to wonder if Sister Paula is still there.

DOORS VERSUS JARS

BY BERNADINE ZIEGLER
(10/30/13)

Doors versus jars, what is the difference besides the obvious in structure, ask yourself this; are they really different at all? Well, let's think this out for a second or two. yes! They come in different sizes, styles, and shapes; they both can be opened and then closed.

When doors become slightly open, they are also called slightly ajar, but when a jar is open, it is just open. Doors open up to a different part of the world, and jars open up with different foods all around the world.

Doors can contain or expose so many things; jars can only expose what is in them. Oh boy! What a pickle. When you open a door you may enter a whole new adventure on life's other side. Open a jar you may just find a tasty treat. I must admit they both sound really neat.

Doors versus jars, which one is really better than the other? Well, you can figure this out, just think. I guess it depends on your sense of adventure or your taste in flavors. If it was my decision I would have to say a door.

Why a door? well you see, a jar just contains what you put in it, and once it's gone its gone, but with a door, it will open up to so many things and places you might actually see a face, but which door do I choose? How about the one that leads to Heaven's Gate, I really like that door! Can a simple jar do that? No! I think not.

EARTHS END OR IS IT?

BY BERNADINE MISURA
(2-25-2001)

My name is Kassy, short for Kassondra, my last name is Gates. I am 9 years of age, the year is 2069, I am not sure of the day or date. I do not know what town or city I am in because as far as the eye can see the earth has been nearly destroyed by a very awful war that never seemed to end. Everywhere devastation, I do not know when or how it got started or even what it was all about because I was born during the war. It is all I know. A lot of people got hurt, men tossing things at each other, men shooting at each other, women, children, animals running for cover things, going boom in the night, and screaming, lots of screaming. And now it is finally quiet after all of these years but where did everyone go? All that I know is that it is now just my Dad and I, his name is Chad, we must find others, please God there has got to be others.

As I was looking around as far as I can see, there is not anything but destruction. I started lifting what I could to see if anyone is under all of this, I heard a noise. I turned around thinking it was my Father, but it was not, it was a very odd looking man a little bigger than I am, he said his name is McFadden, he asked is there anyone, is it just you and me? I said no, my Dad is looking for other survivors; he seemed a little relieved by that. I continued looking around, lifting things, I did not find any people but I did find a very heavy thick large book it is still intact just like it was brand new and it is still white it says the bible on it. I heard of this book before my dad told me once that is a church book but why is it here there is no church as far as I can tell.

McFadden was trying to get my attention. I quickly covered the book up, something told me to, and he asked what is your name child ? I answered Kassy, he said his name again and then said that he is a

Leprechaun Wizard, I did not know what that meant so I had no reaction. He continued to say that he came up to the land world to see if there was anyone alive to tell any stories. He then said we should go find your father because he has to be getting tired and he may need to rest, I agreed. I said lead the way. While McFadden was leading the way, I hurried to uncover the book and took it with me, while he was talking about the path we must take. I thought to myself it is amazing how it went totally undamaged, I love books and I love to read and as I looked around all there was is books totally unreadable, I just wanted to cry this is a special find indeed it was like finding that buried treasure that the pirates always went on about for that one moment I felt just like one of them.

I caught up with McFadden, he was still talking and I struggled to hold on to the book he noticed and said as he stopped what is this you have child? I did not answer because he has the book in his hands and he has it opened, he said it is the Bible he was still looking at it and said it is amazing that it is unharmed he said this is a rare find indeed, he asked where did you find this? I still did not answer he said no matter we must put it in a safe place he motioned his hands around and said some words I can't understand he was saying too low to hear, then the book was gone I was shocked and I nearly screamed where is the book I found? He said it is safe he also said it was too heavy to carry all this way through all this rubble, we must catch up with your father now and just a few miles more we saw a building at least part of one and dad came out and said finally another face to look at before I could say anything dad said Kassy are you alright!? I motioned yes! He went on to say I found someone else she came out and she had a dog with her she said her name is Lauri, and the dogs is Rosco, I was happy to see them. I said father this is McFadden he is a leprechaun wizard dad did not seem like that was out of the ordinary so he shook his hand and dad said to the wizard my name is Joshua Gates. McFadden said we must keep moving the light will be going down soon. I noticed how

McFadden did not like the dog but dad asked how are we going to cover all this ground and rubble before sun down? McFadden thought for a minute and said some more words that none of us understood then a machine appeared. He said in this.

Then he made the book appear again and said we must put this in a safe so it doesn't get stolen or lost. While looking around we found one in the building and when the book was placed in the safe and locked. McFadden said I don't want to leave this here. I asked if you are a wizard why can't you make the safe disappear and then reappear later? He said there is no time for that we are losing light fast we must find shelter, food, and anyone on the way. My dad said to Lauri our house is fine we can go there and there is plenty of food for the night, will you come with us? She answered yes! If my dog can come with me my house was destroyed, dad said yes of course.

McFadden got in the machine first sat down then turned it on then everyone else got in the dog was last McFadden was going to not let the dog in but I said all living creatures have the right to survive even those that you don't like. McFadden with some disappointment agreed and the dog got in and we glided through all the rubble while dad was telling McFadden about all the ground he covered. He did say that he saw a church cross in the distance but it was too far for him to go on foot. McFadden said we will get indoors for the night and go in the early morning. It didn't take us long in this flying machine to go where we needed to go. It was fun but not for the reason we had to use it, we stopped at Gates Manor, dad got out first opened the door to the back yard everyone went in one by one everyone but Kassy and McFadden.

Kassy and McFadden heard noises then they heard voices, where are they what are they saying? Kassy got down to the ground so she could hear better she said excitedly I hear them they are in the ground there are a lot of them, Joshua was also saying loudly we must get inside the light is nearly gone. After everyone had something to eat including Rosco, they all made it an early night. The morning came on so fast.

So fast it didn't feel like I slept at all McFadden said we must go and retrieve the book, we all got into the glider, and we arrived at the building in a flash.

McFadden noticed the safe was gone he shouted the safe is gone and the book has been stolen, he also asked out loud who stole the safe who could of done this? Everyone was quiet for a moment then we heard voices again but could not see them, Kassy was about to say something, but McFadden put his hand over her mouth and said I need to hear where the voices are coming from. There was some grass exposed towards the back of the building the voices got louder, then the voices appeared they are small people Joshua said McFadden said nay they are fairies, the fairies proceeded in telling McFadden that they took the safe with the book in it one of the fairies said we did not know if anyone was alive above ground, we took the book for protection, McFadden wasn't mad anymore but he did ask the fairy are there any more below ground alive she said everyone who lives below ground just moved down further out of harms way.

The fairy continued to say you are the first ones we have seen above ground the fairies returned the safe and the book back to McFadden and he took the book out, the fairies returned below ground. Then McFadden said we must go to find the location of where the cross leads to, than we left to find the church in the distance that my father saw the night before. It did not take too long of a ride in the glider it was fast and covered a lot of territory my dad said, McFadden responded by saying Aye tis fast. We found the church it is open and so are the doors, on the building it says St. Mary's Mission, and I hear people and music.

We all got out one by one and went into the church, we walked in and I saw some people not enough to fill the church it is a large church there are also a lot of animals in here and I hear some babies in the distance crying. The people who are here are on their knees and chanting, it is beautiful in here so peaceful, then not long a man appeared in a brown robe and a rope around his waist, he said peace be with you all my name is father Fagin, may I be of some service? McFadden didn't answer him he just handed him the book and he did say I think this belongs to you. He looked at McFadden with shock and disbelief he said this was stolen from here in the year 2061 after a comet hit the earth the priest that was here before me was murdered for it his name was father Thomas he did everything he could but they killed him anyway. Father Fagin said I thought I would never see this book again especially not in my life time. I wasn't even sure it survived the war. This proves all is not lost and will never be again.

Kassy interrupted the priest by saying I heard babies crying and I see a lot of animals in here, the father said aye! The mission gives all of God's creatures shelter and food, The father went on to say that now that the book has returned to a house of the Lord all will be right again then the good father kissed the book and held it high above his head with both hands and said a prayer to bless the return of the book and us and for what is left of the living and the passing of the dead. He brought the book down again and motioned us to join the others for more prayers, food and shelter. Then when everything was quiet. Kassy heard laughing and saw smiles among everyone and thought to herself this is the sweetest sound I have heard in a long time since the war Joshua said it is true while holding Kassy by the shoulders, everything is going to be right again, the Father continued to motion us in further.

EMMIE

WRITTEN BY BERNADINE MISURA
10/31/93

The year is 1328 A.D. The day is October 31, most people know it as Halloween, a day of evil but not the Catholic Church, it is oddly a beautiful sunny day in a little town in England called Peace Town. There are children playing happily in the school yard before classes no matter what day it is. Catholic children still go to school or church, so this is like a typical day for the all girls school named St. Anthony, a school for wayward girls and for the nuns of the convent, The Sisters of Perpetual Peace.

On this day about fifteen years ago one of the nuns went out and took a walk around the grounds of St. Anthony to pray and to meditate in prayer with the Lord. This was not just any nun, It was the head nun. Her name was Adelina Charles, better known as Mother Charles, she had finished with prayers and meditations, she heard a baby crying, this alone is odd. The cry of this baby did not sound normal for a baby. So Mother had to look to see where it was coming from. Mother discovered where the crying was coming from, she located it and saw a baby placed on the grounds of the convent but barely on the grounds, the baby was wrapped up in a white blanket, by a tree, and the mother is on the ground. It appears like she is asleep but when the Mother Superior arrived she bent down to check the mother of the child. Mother checked everything including her pulse, the mother did not have one, she must of died after giving birth, Mother Charles thought to herself how long have you been out here alone, she picked the baby up checked it also but the baby appeared very different from the average human baby. This baby is very white not just pale very white, the babies outer structure didn't appear to be quite the same as ours, but the mother to the baby looks just like any of us. This confused Mother Charles greatly, she couldn't help but wonder what the father looks like, where and who is he? Mother took a better look at the child and her face for some reason just didn't look right but everything else appears normal. The baby cried again but not so oddly this time it is almost like the baby knows that someone is holding her, her eyes have not yet opened so Mother Charles can't look into her eyes.

Even though Mother Charles had no idea what she could do for this child she heard the Lord's Voice say to her! Daughter keep this child as your own, raise her as yours. Mother looked up to the light in the sky and motioned her acknowledgement of what she heard the Lord say, Mother whispered you have my word Lord I will do as you say! Mother Superior held the child closer to her heart and walked to the convent quietly so no one will find the child, she went to her catacomb with the child, placed her on the bed for now until she can get some help and supplies for the new foundling, she sat on the bed next to the child and said how am I going to raise you, I need help? A thought came to her she suddenly remembered her station she went to four of her most trusted nuns and took them one by one to her catacomb to see her foundling. She informed the sisters I need this to be hush, hush but I also need your help! The sister asked Mother what are you going to do? She said it is not unusual to take in children who need our help I know this hasn't happened since you all became nuns, but it has and can be done, I need your help in raising her to be a healthy normal child or at least keep this all quiet. Mother Charles asked again will you four help me as my most trusted nuns? The Four said Yes! Mother whatever you ask of us you and the child will receive. The sisters asked Mother Charles what is going to be her name? Mother said just Emmie for now! The sisters left one by one to not tip off the other sisters that something unusual just appeared in the church.

After the four nuns left, there appeared a light in Mother's catacomb. It is a beautiful lady. Mother looked up at the baby's eyes, they opened and they are looking at the light. Mother also looked in that direction it is the Holy Mother Mary, she said to Mother Charles daughter take the child to the bishop and have her protected from any evil that may come her way, have Emmie blessed and inform the bishop that you intend to raise the child as your own, Mother Charles, agreed with the Lady of the Light. After the Lady of the Light left, Mother Charles took Emmie quietly out of the church. The baby made no sound just like baby Jesus. Mother used no vehicles to get around, because she had to take the baby in silence to Bishop Michael, when she arrived at the monastery with the same name as her convent: St. Anthony. The Bishop Michael seemed to know somehow that she was coming with the baby and why. Bishop Michael said Mother I was expecting you to arrive, she said nothing and then the bishop said to her Our Lady informed me and told me to give this child a baptism, Mother said yes! Your Eminence. He said then we must get this done so you can be on your way. Mother bowed and the baptism was performed. Mother Charles took Emmie back to the convent and to her catacomb to find all the things displayed for Emmie to use as she grows up, Mother was overjoyed she asked her most trusted nun Sister Anita, where did it all come from, she said it was all donated by anonymous.

As Emmie grew up through the years she started to develop, her looks more to appear more human, but was she? No one could ever know the truth except for the Lord God, and He wasn't telling. The Four sisters and Mother Charles were totally responsible for all her education and from what I know she excelled in her studies. Emmie was going to be fifteen on Halloween and she is more than ready to go to high school with the rest of the wayward girls of Peace Town, Mother did worry so much about this because of her appearance but Sister Anita, whispered to Mother don't worry she is God's child just like the rest of them she will be strong and if she becomes weak she still has us to come to, don't worry we will watch over her. Emmie will be fine you'll see! Sister Anita also said to Mother besides just look at her, her skin is a light brown now and she is much taller than the other girls at her age her eyes are now a clouded green but yes! Her hair is still white and she has freckles all over her face. Mother Charles couldn't stop looking at Emmie and crying, Sister Anita whispered again Mother she will be fine!

The day finally came, it is a sunny August day, Mother Charles did as always walk the grounds in the morning, prayed in silence to the Lord but this time she also prayed to the Holy Mother to watch over Emmie. And this day Mother got up walked to the school to see how many girls are here this year? There are fourteen, the most they ever had and with Emmie added this year she makes fifteen girls. Before classes started the girls played in the school yard. Emmie was already out there before the others arrived so she can learn to socialize with others, then the bell rang, the Sisters introduced themselves to the children and then said to the girls we say a prayer first before we start everyday the prayer is the prayer of St. Anthony: the name on the school building, they all bowed down and chanted Oh! Holy Saint Anthony, Gentlest Of Saints, Your Love For God And Charity For His Creatures Made You Worthy, When On Earth, To Possess Miraculous Powers. Encouraged by This Thought, I Implore You To Obtain For Me (Request). Oh Gentle And Loving St. Anthony Whose Heart Was Ever Full Of Human Sympathy, Whisper My Petition Into The Ears Of The Sweet Infant, Jesus, Who Loved To Be Folded In Your Arms; And The Gratitude Of My Heart Will Ever Be. Amen. The bell rang again for the classes to start. All the children came in without any fuss for now, sighed the sisters. All the girls took their seats and in the front row were two sisters, fraternal twins Danielle, and Merilee, also Emmie so the sister nuns can keep an eye on her, in all the classes of the day and lunch also went off without a hitch yes! There were some glances but nothing to worry about. The sisters sighed again, then the recess bell rang the girls all divided to their chosen spots Emmie was the only one who didn't know anyone else so she was a little stand offish she could even hear what others could be saying about anything at all times. To Emmie this is a down fall. She heard a girl speak about Emmie's odd appearance but not cruel, but it still made Emmie a little uncomfortable, she looked at the sisters at the door and bowed and sat down right next to Merilee, who is the girl remarking on Emmie's appearance, Emmie said hello just like any other child would. Danielle was very pleasant with Emmie but Merilee started asking questions of Emmie about her background and appearance this did make Emmie stand offish still but Emmie answered all she could when Merilee was asking about Emmie's parents this just made her want to cry her mother died from birth and her father wasn't around this made Emmie very sad that she can't remember anything, she wanted to go hide somewhere but she knew she had to be strong, Emmie said to Merilee the truth about her parents and said that Mother Charles is her mother now, Danielle and Merilee were a little surprised by this, Merilee asked some offensive questions such as what planet do you come from what are your people like? Emmie just wanted to hide she had no idea how to answer, but she didn't know how or where she could go but she did find a place the more Emmie gets stressed or sad a strange feeling comes over her like pains in her back and shoulders, she was developing wings, kind of in a the shape of butterfly wings, she needed to talk with Mother but the bell rang for classes again Emmie had to hide them real fast, she heard Danielle say to Merilee you were out of line why are you asking such mean questions don't you realize that you were hurting her? There was no response from Merilee she just shrouded her shoulders, Emmie just wanted to run away but there was no- where for her to go she started turning into a butterfly like appearance she was very scared she didn't know what to do. She knew somehow she had to get back to her human like appearance some- how she did.

School resumed everything went back to normal as normal as could be for Emmie, the classes went off again with no hitch. The school bell rang again to end the day. Some of the girls lingered in the school grounds, Emmie went out to talk to them including Merilee and Danielle, Danielle tried to apologize on behalf of her sister but Merilee stood up and said no! She wanted to apologize for herself. She said quietly, I am sorry if I made you sad or uncomfortable I didn't mean to it's just I ask a lot of questions and I forget about how they may hurt someone she whispered again please accept my apology please! Emmie smiled and said it's okay I understand that I don't look like all of you and that may make you also a little uncomfortable. Then Emmie asked a question but are all of us really exactly the same? Before Merilee could answer, Emmie said while still smiling we are all a little different that is what makes us who we are, we are all God's creation right? Merilee didn't know what to say she held her head down as to say I am ashamed of my behavior but Emmie said no worries! But somehow Emmie knew this wasn't the end of it, and this made her a little sad for Peace Town, Emmie went to Mothers catacomb to wait for her so she can tell mother about her day. Emmie knew mother would be interested in anything that will and can happen to her in school. Mother Charles is the only mother she has ever known, and the sisters are the only sisters she may ever have.

Mother did come to her and ask her in a gentle whisper and a gentle embrace so how was school did anything happen? Emmie knew what this question meant Emmie said mother don't get upset but yes! A girl did ask me some off-color questions yes! They did make me sad and uncomfortable, but I spoke to her anyway she didn't or doesn't mean anything by her questions, she is just inquisitive and she always needs to ask questions at least that is what her sister Danielle tells me, and she is a nice girl, so I must believe her, and then Emmie paused a little and in a whisper told mother something else happened to me today: I started to form wings like a butterfly. Could you imagine how mother felt by hearing this news? She was shocked in silence for Emmie, Emmie went on with this incident. Mother could hear the tears in her lungs. Mother, what is happening to me? I am scared why is this happening to me? Mother Charles explained everything to

Emmie about how she was found that Halloween day almost fifteen years ago and how she also found her mother dead right next to her and that there was no father to be found but mother also said your birth mother had a locket on her and Mother Charles kept it with her all the time to not risk anyone finding out about Emmie, mother held it up in the air and said this is yours, Emmie gently took it from her and opened it up, There is a picture. Emmie said she looks just like me: she is beautiful, mother whispered yes! She is and so are you. Emmie couldn't stop looking at the picture then mother took it from her to place on her neck and said wear this always and always remember her! Emmie noticed that there is another picture in the locket she looked at it and smiled she said Mother this is you Mother whispered with tears in her throat yes! Emmie will you keep me with you also? Emmie smiled and said yes! Mother always! I will treasure you and this locket always!

Emmie said Mother I am still so scared what do I do if this happens again? she thought for a second, get to a safe place: quiet and alone and then do your changing. Mother asked Emmie, can you feel when this changing is going to happen do you have some warning? Can you change back to a human appearance when this happens? Emmie said, I'm not sure, it just started today but I was able to change back. Emmie said again in a whisper Mother I'm so scared! mother held her again and said dry your eyes Emmie God will always be with you: after all He did tell me to find you and He did tell me to have you baptized by the bishop, mother said if for some reason you can't find me and the sisters can't either: go to Bishop Michael he will know and be able to help! Okay? Emmie shook her head to acknowledge what mother said Mother dabbed her tears away and said don't worry you have God and us here for you and then mother hugged her for a long while after they both sat down on one of the beds. Mother whispered lie down and take a nap: you had a hard day I'll call you for supper. Emmie laid down and mother pulled a blanket over her and then closed the door behind her quietly, then went to her office for more answers to Emmie's questions that haven't been asked yet.

It is another gorgeous sunny day just like yesterday, Mother was praying to God late into the night: I think it was for me, I'm not sure if she even came to bed, but the school bell was about to ring for another day of school but Mother Charles doesn't need to worry, all the teachers said good morning to all the girls and I, another day of school went off without a hitch, this day during a recess time all the girls came to talk to me and Merilee was still a little harsh with the questions but not as bad as yesterday, but *I* sensed something happening to me again I remembered what mother told me to have a safe place and I did, this one took a while I became a full butterfly, I even flew over everyone I was able to hear everything that the girls were saying about everybody, I flew around one more time then I felt changing again I saw that Danielle was alone so I went over to her after I became a human form.

I sat down next to Danielle on a gray park bench I asked Danielle does Merilee not like me for some reason? Danielle said no not at all, she is just trying to be your friend now, but she fears that you are mad at her or you hate her, I was shocked, and I feared that my wings would pop out. one of the sisters came out with a cape for me to wear so I can hide my wings in plain sight with no one to know the wiser, I stood up and put the cape on and Sister Anita said, my goodness girl you are growing fast and very tall much taller than the other girls! I looked at the sister out of shock and she caught on and covered her quickly, mother went back into the school all I could think is Thank God it was just Danielle and me all the other girls went home. I sat back down Danielle said she stayed back because she wanted to speak to me on be-half of Merilee and she wanted to make sure I wasn't unhappy. I said that is very kind of you Danielle. Thank you but you need not worry, I like your sister Merilee, you and all the other girls, but I did ask Dan-ielle how do you all feel about me after all I am the new kid in Peace

Town and on the block? Danielle waved her hand and said your cool I like you too, and it's awesome that mother took you in as her daughter also, I couldn't stop smiling, I never heard those kind words before.

Peace Town England, St. Anthony's school for wayward girls had the best year for their girls in a long time. In fact, all the girls graduated when they were all the age of twenty except for Emmie, they graduated in June before Emmie's twentieth Birthday. Danielle went on to become a lawyer, Merilee, went to become a business woman, and Emmie did leave the convent to experience a life outside of it but the sisters and Mother Charles helped her every step of the way, Emmie went on to help other children that people didn't want because they were different in some way. Mother didn't want to let Emmie go and there were many nights mother prayed and cried for her Emmie, but she knew she had to learn about the outside world also to become an all around person.

Emmie always remembered something Danielle always said to her you can be anything you want to be and don't let anyone tell you differently: and this Emmie told to every child she placed with a good family, Danielle got married shortly after school let out, she had a baby girl, Danielle's husband died shortly after Rory was born, she raised her on her own and sometimes she called Emmie for help. Merilee wasn't happy with her life, she got bored with it so she asked Mother Charles if she could join the sisterhood of the Sisters of Perpetual Peace, Let's just say Mother was surprised but pleased. Merilee's new name is now Sister Bertilla Attalas, When Rory became the age of twenty and Danielle is now forty five, Danielle joined the convent also. Rory a couple of years later followed suit with her true mother, Danielle's name is Sister Basilla Chantal, and Rory's new name is Sister Blandina Mary, they only see each other in passing.

Emmie was going to get married and Mother Charles was so happy that she found a husband so she can learn how to be a wife to someone, Emmie had a beautiful wedding with all the nuns and the Bishop. Bishop Michael was the one that married her to her now husband. He is a doctor who helps the poor. Doctor William Malcolm Benise, Emmie had a baby boy while William, was helping some poor refugees, and he got killed by a flying knife that was intended for someone else. Emmie was devastated by the news and she just had their son, William Augustine Benise.

Emmie didn't know how to be a mother, so she went to the convent and asked Sister Anita, what can she do? Emmie told her, I want my son to become a priest but I fear for his life, the sister said we can take him to Bishop Michael, He will know what we can do. The Bishop said I can take the child and raise him on a few conditions. One: you become a nun just like Mother Charles, Two: you give up your son to the church, and Three: you may see him but only as a sister and not on constant occasions. Emmie said with some defeat in her voice and her head held down: Yes! Your Eminence I will do as you ask for my son but may I ask you one more thing? The Bishop said in a quiet tone, ask! She said, Your Eminence may I have updates on his progress as he grows through the years and that you will tell him everything? The Bishop gestured a yes!

Emmie did get constant growth updates on her son, but she was careful not to tell him anything but she wanted to, Emmie got to see him become a priest, he is now called Father Augustine of the Dominicans, Emmie was so proud a few years back. Emmie lost Mother Charles, she went to Heaven but now Emmie is in her sixties, and she isn't feeling so good she went to her catacomb to slow down, but it didn't help. she laid down closed her eyes to never wake. Father Augustine was outside with a parishioner, and he looked up in the sky and saw a beautiful light racing across the sky, the Father heard about these lights they come from Gods Angels His messengers, they take a soul straight to heaven, Father couldn't take his eyes off the racing light and he whispered, Safe journey my Mother! I love you and will always miss you, with a tear in his eye a sister came to him and delivered Emmie's locket to him. the sister said your mother Sister Ursulina Mary Vitalis, wanted you to have this when she passed. The locket now also has her picture in the locket with a message always remember me my son. I love you.

GOD'S ASSISTANT

BY BERNADINE ZIEGLER
(3-5-13)

This was originally an answering machine message that I wrote out of frustration from too many phone calls, but God Asked me to write it this way instead, I hope and pray He Thinks it's more than okay, here it goes, Lord. Oh! My Humility, God Forgive me. I pray I will someday be His Assistant.

The message started out by me saying: This is God's Assistant, if you are calling for God because you think you deserve to go to Heaven, press # One, if you are calling God because you know you deserve Purgatory, press # Two, if you want to talk to God, because you know you deserve to go to hell, then press # Six, three times, I see you pressed the # Six, three times, then you need not talk to me. This call has ended, Good-bye!!

When I first wrote out this message, I just couldn't stop laughing, to this day I still think it's funny, but think of it this way as I have been: When you really break it down, it isn't really funny anymore, I think of all the evil being done in this world today, and all the sins being committed against the Lord. Are we all really this blind? How did we become so blind?

I think long and hard to myself, how many people really think it's this easy to get to Heaven, or Purgatory? We must understand it's not easy to get into Heaven or even Purgatory, we have to Love and Serve the Lord and accept the fact that He is our Lord God the Almighty. Before this can happen, it's always easy to go to hell. How many people would not press the # Six, but they really deserve # Six?

We all have to understand, it's not our decision where we are going to end up. It's God's Judgment that makes the call, it's the sins we commit on Earth Against God, that really does us in. Our Judgment Day is every day of our lives, nay! God's Lives, our final days are when we receive the verdict of whether He will make or break our fall; you make the call that is all.

GOD'S FLASHLIGHTS

BY MARK EDWARD ZIEGLER
9-22-2013
INSPIRED BY BERNADINE, HIS WIFE.

THE STARS ARE GOD'S FLASHLIGHTS, MAKING SURE AND CARING FOR THIS WORLD THE WAY HE PLANNED IT.

THE STARS ARE HIS ANGELS, HIS HEAVENLY HELPERS, FOR THEY ARE THE COMFORTERS WHEN THINGS GO AWRY WITH ONE OF HIS CHILDREN.

WHEN SOMEONE UNFORTUNATELY PASSES AWAY, PEOPLE ARE SO SAD TO HEAR ABOUT THE PASSING, AND THEY MAKE THE COMMENT HE DIED ALONE. NO, HE DID NOT. AN ANGEL IS ALWAYS THERE TO HELP THIS PERSON GO INTO THE AFTER LIFE.

GOD PLANNED THE COURSE OF THIS ONCE BEAUTIFUL WORLD RANGING FROM ADAM AND EVE TO MOTHER THERESA. HE HOWEVER IS NOT SURPRISED BY THE TURN OF EVENTS THROUGHOUT HISTORY. THAT IS WHY ONE DAY HE IS GOING TO SNAP HIS FINGERS AND SAY "THAT'S IT" "YOU MESSED UP MY WORLD LONG ENOUGH!" THEN ALL THE LIGHTS WENT OUT...

THIS IS WHY GOD HAS ANGELS, THE HEAVENLY FLASHLIGHTS, HE CAN BE EVERYWHERE. BUT CHOSES NOT TO BE.

TO ALL GRANDPARENTS

BY BERNADINE MISURA
(8-25-06)

To all grandmas: including my grandmother, and all the grandmothers of the past, most especially for the grandmas of all the saints, I want to say a heartfelt thank you for everything you do, for the ones that passed on, God will always be with you. You do so much for us such as: raise your children and then you help them with their children while sitting idly by, when your daughter or son needs your help, there you are.

Grandfathers, I can't leave you out: just when things get out of hand and everyone is turning quite mad, there you are to make a stand. You put out your hand and shout stop! And somehow with you, everything seems to just work out, to all you grandfathers of saints, and all alike, I give you a heartfelt thank you, as for my grandfather, I'm sorry I don't remember you, but my love for you is just as true blue.

This is for all the grandparents who were parents themselves, I thank you for always being there no matter what you have or had gone through, Thank you for helping us to grow up and help us figure our world out, and maybe someday we will be as good as you at the job you do. Thank you, God Bless You.

HE WAS ALWAYS THERE

BY BERNADINE MISURA
(7-27-06)

When I was about four years of age, I was already in a terrible way, I was even in a hospital metal bed cage, at times when I got out, and I went home. No! I did not roam; I had a whole lot of things to figure out, such as: who are my parents? What is my name? Who are these other kids? Did I dare ask of any ones help? Did I even ask God, Are You There? No, I did not really have a care, but He was there.

Did I ask anyone what is wrong with me? Or did I ask why I was in a strange place in a locked bed for my head? No! Instead, I stayed quiet and never said a thing, until I needed something, No! I did for some reason want to die, I did not know why? But He was still there.

Through all my trials, and tribulations, I still somehow ended up in school, I don't know how without knowing my name, I don't remember a thing, I didn't even know I was an epileptic, or even what that meant, I do know if I was told back when I was young the information is for sure all gone. But he was still there.

When I got healthier, and became more aware, I just didn't figure out all the stuff I went through, I even remember all of my attempts at suicide, four in all, He said, One more time I cannot be at your side, and you will take a great fall. I beg for mercy, I ask that you have pity, I was not aware that you were there. He Said I was always there. I said I didn't know anyone cared.

He said again, I was always there watching over you, I still will be, If you listen to Me. Listen to My Plea, You must get confirmed; I need you to learn to Love Me so you can be free to be with Me. He was always there and can be for you. This is true no matter what you may go through it's up to you.

HEAVEN'S GATE

BY BERNADINE MISURA
(7-21-06)

Heaven's Gate I wonder who really decides our fate, is it I? Do I decide
which path to take? No *I don't think so! Thinking this way you surely
Don't know which way to go. Yes! It's true we were given free choice
This I know. But if you don't choose the right path, do you really have the
right to have a voice? I must admit this was my choice but something just
didn't seem to fit, what was it? What could it be, it's not
Up to me? When I figured this out, He came to me.*

*Who is He? Is it the guardian of Heaven's Gate? No I don't think so, Could
it be the Lord Our God, Above? I thought to myself, yes! It does sound like
He. I ask why me, Lord? Why me? He answered because I Love You Unconditionally. I asked how could this be? I beg you have Mercy on me. If you pray
and pray, everything will be okay.*

*When you Pray to God, every day you will definitely find the right way
He holds the Key to Heaven's Gate; He Decides our fate.*

*For all sinners' it's not too late to know who you are. I beg you to not stray too
far away, from God, Christ, and the Blessed Trinity, Because if you do, well I
guess that choice is up to you, as for me, I choose the Blessed Three of the Holy
Trinity, I want to at least go to Purgatory, I just want you to know hell, is not
the path to take. Beg for His Mercy and Forgiveness, open up to God's Love
from Above.*

*Show Him that you Love Him too, It's the right thing to do, just let the
Lord's Love Flow, believe me with His Love for you and in you. Life will
never look so blue. I will pray for you, if you prefer the hotter way to hell,*

well! Only time will tell. Oh, how you will miss out on Heavens Delight, Oh, what a fright!

Ask yourself this question, what do you have if you don't have His Love, or Humility? The answer is nothing! The sinners who choose to receive His Love and Pity. The feeling is like watching the Flight of His White Dove. God is the Perfect and Only Love, for me.

So again I ask this question, who really decides your fate through Heaven's Gate? When you choose His Grace you are a sinner but still a winner, with His Love you will always have a place in His Heart, I Pray that You and I will never part. His Love for us is Tried and True, you know what to do, when you choose the Right Path, you can do no wrong, just don't wait too long.

HIS HOLY BIBLE

BY BERNADINE ZIEGLER
(6/17/15)

There are so many different books out here. Which one is the right one? Why are there so many different versions of His Holy Words? Which one is really His Holy Bible? Tell me which one do I follow? How will I ever be able to tell the difference between them all? I really want to know the answer because I love Him and I wish never to take an awful fall. Please, is there someone out here that can tell the difference or does anyone really care that they may be doing wrong sinning and falling from His Grace? I ask you why, why don't you care, you don't want to see His Beautiful Place, why? Why would you want that to happen to you? That would make me feel so blue, why doesn't it you?

What is His Holy Bible? What does it contain? What does it all mean? What does the word Bible really mean? Well, from what I understand which isn't much, is that the word bible means good story, His Story. I'm guessing that would be His Diary, but also what I have heard the word B.I.B.L.E. means the Basic Instructions Before Leaving Earth, but what does it contain? Stories that were written by His Apostles, and Prophets while they traveled with Him. The Old Testament is the set-up of God's Plans and the people who are chosen by Him to cast His Graces On. The New Testament is the work of God's Son Jesus, The King of all. Everything that He spoke, every place He trod, everything He did was written by His chosen Men to document everything.

How to tell the correct Bible is to find His Holy Church. The one He said to St. Peter The Rock, upon you I build my church, which today is the Roman Catholic Church, a lot of you out here don't want to hear that because you think your church was the first, but if you are not a church created by The Lord Jesus you are not His church and you do not follow His Written Words, His Written words were published shortly after His Resurrection, which He has set us free. If you follow any books written by anyone else such as the King James, all churches that follow this book is following a man-made church, not His church, I will always pray for you all, because a lot of you have no idea. Or you chose to understand that this man (John Smith) took the Holy Words of our Bible, the Catholic Bible and cut it into pieces and then added his own words, wouldn't this be plagiarism?

Plagiarism: which means copying or taking parts from one writing and attaching some words of your own. Are you all who follow these fake bibles aren't you following a plagiarist? Isn't this a crime to plagiarize so I ask why haven't these fake bible writers been charged with something and for those who follow these books, I simply ask why, why would you follow evil and evil doers or even enter into their churches? These are not God's Houses nor will they ever be: why would anyone not want to be with the Lord in His Father's House? Don't you all understand He Loves you? He loves us all, why don't you want to receive His Grace? Why don't you want to see His Holy Face in His Daddy's place, what is wrong with you? Now you know The True Bible, The True Word, what are you going to do, are you still going to follow evil or you going to follow the Truth, the one that loves you?

HIS HOLY FLAME

BY BERNADINE ZIEGLER

(2-9-13)

His Holy Flame, His Holy Light, how is it you keep on burning so bright even through human plight, what feeds Your Flame? Somehow Your Flame burns all day and Your Stars light up the night, what feeds His Holy Flame? Ever Lasting Love is His Name.

Oh! God, I beg of you to Light my hearts flame to save me from evils stain and pain, please wash all my cares away with Your Rain. Oh God, I ask of You to Light the Fires within me so I may yearn for Your Everlasting Love, please Lord Share Your Love with me. Oh, how I Love Thee, Teach Me Humility, to help me get through.

Neither shining star, candle light, burning flame, do you even know my name? No matter who or what you are, none of us would have life if it weren't for His Strife, Oh! Why is it that I can stand or sit here just yearning for his Eternal Light, no matter day or night?

No matter what you call Him: Holy Father, Yahweh, The Blessed Trinity, in Him there are Three. The Holy Ghost; the lover of most, The Holy Spirit, I pray someday we will share it, and the Holy Father, there can be no other: He Cleanses us through His Holy Host, who we need the most, Lord of all, and I am He, God Almighty, they're all the same, but without His Everlasting Reign there would be no us, this you can trust.

Just remember this, He Loves and Forgives us for our sins, so I ask you to Love Him too. He and I ask of you to do, it's up to you. Get on your knees, and say, Please God, Save Me. Please Lord, may I have some of

Your Holy Flame to soothe my pain, my obedience to You will always be true, His Love for me will always sustain, and get me through.

HIS HOLY SCEPTER

BY BERNADINE ZIEGLER
(1-27-13)

His Holy Scepter, God's Holy Light, Oh! How does it burn so bright? Who is the keeper? Oh how I have so many questions for you, are You One of His Chosen Vessels, the guardian of His Holy Grace? Do you use His Holy Scepter, to tame or destroy evils face, I wonder is that really up To You? Tell me true.

My God, what is it you ask of me to do? I am here for you. Maybe to show evil where to go. Please God, don't let me go. My love for You will always grow, with His Eternal Light, may my soul take flight day and night, with His Mercy, Guidance and Love; maybe I will see a White Dove from Above. Won't that be a delight?

I pray every day to the Lord Above please save me Oh Lord, with Your Love. Please cleanse me of my many sins, the ill repressed, from within, I pray every day maybe just to say, Hey! If that is okay. I'm so very sorry; I haven't given it my best save me oh! Lord, from evils unrest.

The Guardian of Your Holy Scepter, Your Chosen will shine Your Holy Light, through my breast so my soul can take its rest with other delights. He will Touch my face with your Holy Grace, even in this place of disgrace. When God will call me I will simply say yes! Lord it's me. I'm Unworthy of Thee, I beg of You Mercy, Save my soul from evils toll, I pray every day to You, so the devil will not have any control of my soul, so I ask Lord, what is it You want of me? What can I possibly do for Thee? Please Lord, from You and Your Blessed Church, I'll never stray, not even for a day, even when evil tells me it's okay! I love you Lord, and will always Obey.

You ask who is the real guardian of His Holy Light, who is the Keeper of His Holy Scepter? The answer is: one of His Chosen, unless His Holy Bonds are broken, then we will be Judged and turned into dust. I pray someday it will be for all of us who makes the choice to have a voice, to stand up for His Holy Truth, and to share in His Love and Grace, and maybe see His Holy Face, in my favorite place. I am always at peace even with His Nuns, and Priests, to say the least. Who I love and admire they really do inspire, me to see how wonderful it can all be for you and me. To be a receiver of His Holy Scepter it really cannot get any better.

HOLY MARY

BY BERNADINE ZIEGLER
(12/12/14)

Holy Mary, Mother of God, Pray for us sinners, every time you say these words don't you ever wonder why? Why Her? Why do we ask Her to pray for us, why do we need Her Help, why do we need help at all? Well I must confess I felt this way. I asked myself these questions when I was young, I am older now I do have the answer, let's think this out: so you will understand as I do now and be able show others The Way, as I will show you, and as The Holy Mother, and Jesus Her Son has shown me.

Just like every day in her young life she did what was asked of her, for this reason she had no sin, and also because she herself was not born with sin not to mention she remained a virgin so God Kept Her as Chosen. One day an Angel named Gabriel came to Her and said, you will bear a Child, and she said how can this be? I don't know man. A Holy Child, a Son; and you shall call Him Jesus, don't you ever wonder what you would do if this happened to you, I do? Can you really imagine?

Holy Mary, I'm sure had some fear but she also said, Your Will be done! I wonder, if you would have answered that way, would you surrender to God? I must admit I'm not sure I would have, May God forgive me, but ask yourself what would you do? Holy Mary was also told by the Angel Your Son will be King of Heaven but after His Resurrection to set us all free. I wonder how you would feel about this information, just what would you do if you would have said no! Thank you? Can you imagine?

When Mary was pregnant with child and she was not married: can you imagine how Joseph was feeling, one can only imagine. Just remember women were stoned for this. Would you of had acceptance like Joseph did and marry her anyway and vowed to take care of a baby that wasn't his or yours, could you and would you have done this and then took Mary to safety to have the Holy Baby and to fulfill a Prophecy. And can you imagine doing this for God, would you have done this for God?

This is why she is and always will be the Holy Mother of God, I ask you how would you feel if you knew the Baby you Gave Birth to will die by Crucifixion for us sinners, perfect strangers do we really deserve this? What would you do with this information knowing you have to live through this, and just watch it happen to go through all of His Pain with Him, can one really imagine this, as for me I say no! I don't think so. I never want to imagine this. Don't you all see She Loves us just as much as God and Jesus, this you don't need to imagine, you just need to understand and say thank you.

Through all the Pains of the Stations of the Cross which also contain a prayer. I think they are from Her while experiencing everything with Jesus, all through this the Birth, Crucifixion, Death and Resurrection! Did anyone see how She was feeling or even how She was coping; did anyone see Her experience all of His Pains? She had to be strong for all of us; I think we all should all say Thank You Holy Mary Mother of God, please pray for us.

Let's not forget she even created a way to speak and pray to Her Son- the Holy Rosary- yes! They are a Mystery but the True Mystery is how, when, you pray with the Rosary if it really does open the door to Heavens Blue Light, I just wonder, how does He hear us pray with these Beautiful Strings of Beads, I also wonder how did She know, that people on earth would really pray with these Strings of Beads that can and do so much for us.

All I can say is Thank You Holy Mother for showing us The Way, Thank You for loving me as much as I do You. Please say a prayer for me. We all should pray the Holy Rosary at least once a day and also pray to The Holy Mother so She will Intercede for us, Oh! How wondrous a blessing that is bestowed upon us.

I DON'T LIKE

WRITTEN BY BERNADINE ZIEGLER
ON 8-19-08

I know I never have to like other people's decisions that they make for their lives, but when they involve others that is when I form my opinion, I don't like people in the business world who always try to be politically correct, who are you trying to fool? I also don't like those business slogans that say they are equal opportunity employers, what are you trying to prove, you are not equal at all. I know I have worked at many of these businesses, and they never keep the real American, the Native American, which is me.

I don't like those adults who tell their kids lies to cover up their own faults, or those adults who act like children themselves and go to bars and get into fights, even with a knife, I would say that is intent to kill, I really don't like when they claim temporary insanity, well I got one question for you if you were or are insane you wouldn't know whatever you do is wrong, so you can't be insane at anytime if you know you did the crime, therefore you must do the time, and why do the courts accept this plea? Are the judge and jury really this lazy?

I used to like truckers until I got hit by one and he tried to say it was my fault and make me pay, to you I say go far, far, away from me, as for democrat, liberal, part-time republicans, cradle Catholics, and ones who claim to be catholic for convenience, and all who do crimes against God because they want a good time, and they want to change or destroy all of God's Work, well I really can't stand you, how dare you? Who do you think died and gave you the right? Go ahead and say it. I dare you!

I ALWAYS REMEMBER TO THANK GOD

BY BERNADINE MISURA

(11-13-06)

I always remember to thank the Lord Above for His Guidance, His forgiveness, but most of all His Love. I thank him for everything He does for me and everything He doesn't do for me, even when He says no! I say you are the best! Who would know what I want or really need?

God has done so many things for me, in spite of all the sins, and tribulations, believe me, if He wasn't there for me, I know for sure there would be no jubilation. Even when I have had a bad day, He says, my child, everything will be okay.

God gives me so many gifts, and many blessings, by His Holy Grace, I know I will never be able to repay, for this reason I always remember to thank God, every night and day. I pray this is how to tell Him how much you love Him, I think we should get down on our knees and pray and say to Him thank you Lord, for always being there, even when we think our lives are in disrepair.

So you see, He doesn't care about the undone things we have promised him or accomplished any of our goals, He just loves us regardless of our hopes and dreams, these don't mean anything to him. He just wants us to follow and Love Him despite these things. I will always remember to thank God, how about you? I'll even pray with you.

I WILL FORGIVE YOU

BY BERNADINE MISURA
(9/19/06)

This is for all you sinners, who have trespassed against me.
I know this is written in the Bible but let this be known, as
a human, this is very hard to say and do. I stand up with
Open arms and whisper. I will forgive you.

I know God Loves me and you too, but you still have to ask
For His Forgiveness, not just to be clean of your sins, but for
The Peace, Joy, and Love God will Give us if we give Him our
Pledge of Love as He Did for you and me.

By God's Will as our Holy Father does for us, I know He will
Forgive you to as I do, I know this to be true, because I'm a sinner
Too, and I Love You. Let's not forget that He sent His Only Son.

I WON'T GO TO HELL FOR YOU

WRITTEN BY MARK ZIEGLER
DECEMBER 12, 2014

Eternal separation from God is a very sad thing for both He and I. Sad for Him because he has to send away one of the children created by Him. Sad for me because my soul would not do what He wanted to obtain Eternal salvation.

Never to see His Face. Never to be in His Arms. HOW VERY SAD!

When we got married, I promised to love, honor, cherish my bride. I did not promise to go to hell for you. That is a deep, dark place. Blacker than the darkest night. I would like to be in heaven dancing with the angels. Hopefully, you atheists and agnostics are listening to God's words!

The Most High Father has asked me to endure many things, going to hell is not one of them. That is one thing I will not do for anyone.

My wife is a very unique woman. Being with her under the Almighty God forever and ever is the greatest gift I could ever obtain. My goodness, I would get on the heavenly elevator and ask, where is my wife?

But if He does say, "depart from me, for I never knew you". Then we got a problem. Eternal pain is something I cannot bear.

I believe that I am bound for purgatory. At least I have a shot at heaven. So I can't blow this. The word "defeat" is not in my vocabulary. Never has been, never will be.

I don't have enough information on the place of the eternally damned, but I do not want to explore further, DO YOU?

ALWAYS SEEK HIM ON THE CROSS

BY BERNADINE MISURA

When I needed a best friend while I suffered Oh! So much

Sometimes you are down on your luck and you're seriously thinking of committing suicide because of the trouble with the family, that does bring on a very quiet depression just as I have gone through I had no idea of what to do or have someone to talk to, I suffered in my loneliness with no one there to care, while I was in my quiet despair.

I would like to give you some advice since I survived by
Seeing His Holy Light, I know things seem really tough
And your world is turning upside down I ask you to not
Give up; don't give into the evils pain.

I know things will seem like they will only get a little rough just hang on when Your world turns black remember to always seek Him on The Cross remember what he did for you he loves you this much it Is true.

Remember if you ask him, He will always take care of you
I promise this please don't be blue, He is here for you to just like me.
In good times and bad if you seek him on the cross there can never be any loss.

So please don't worry. This is my advice to you because I went through it too. I always Seek Him on The Cross, each and every day I pray you will to, so what do you say?

I'LL NEVER FORGET

BY BERNADINE MISURA
(8-18-06)

This is for all who die by no choice of their own; they were removed from their home, never to see the sight of light by someone yet unknown. Your family always sitting by the phone, waiting for someone or something to bring back home from whoever took you, shame on you, who are you? We'll never know but you are not alone, you I'll never forget even though we never met.

For all of those who touched my heart, from you God will never part and for all that stood by me even when others tried to hurt me emotionally or denied me for what reasons I'll never know, but for all of you, I thank you and will never forget you. I just wanted you all to know I will always love you even when God calls you home.

Now as for all of you who have tried to eliminate God from all our lives, and to remove all the good that He has done in this world for everyone, for you may God's Justice be done. For those of you who decide that it's wrong for God, Jesus and Mary to be known or shown to me or for all to see I have one question for you.

How dare you? How could you be so callous? What or who really caused you malice? That is our religious right given to us by God. No! It is not your decision to make; it's ours and ours alone. For you I say shame on you for everything you do, I, most of all, will never forget the destruction, and dysfunction, you cause and do.

This for all my friends I have lost along the way, especially my school friends that died in Desert Storm, there is so many of you, I think of you often. Then I can't help feeling sorry for you and feeling so alone but I also know you all chose this mission and your positions, to stand up for our rights, the gift of their lives for ours will never go unforgotten and their presence should never go unknown, you are all heroes to me, and always will be.

Most of all, this is for all the soldiers who stand up for our rights and to save our lives from evils strife, and to the fall so we can have justice for all. Let's have a moment of silence to show them that we care, love and thank them for everything they do for us, you will always be in God's and my heart, I will never forget you, this is and they are true red white and blue, God Bless You.

I'M ALWAYS CHASING
HIS HOLY RAINBOW

BY BERNADINE ZIEGLER
(10/6/15)

Have you ever seen His Holy Rainbow? Have you ever seen what you call a rainbow in the sky? Don't you ever wonder how is it formed? Who picked such beautiful colors and how do they touch each other but not run together, where does it start and where does it end? Some people say that at the end of a rainbow you will find a pot of gold. Don't you wonder how they know, did they ever find the end of the rainbow and how did they make it back to their family and friends? Will one ever discover the solution? Well how about this notion for a solution: I say it is God's Will God's message to us to let us know He is there, He will always care. Rainbows are a message of encouragement to tell you everything is okay, everything is going to be okay.

How does the rainbow connect with God you ask? Well, let's think about this. I think that it is mentioned in the book of Revelation. I think in 10:1-11 where it mentions a mighty angel with an open scroll and how he arrives on a cloud with a rainbow over his head, but what do the colors mean, why were these colors chosen? I've have been doing some research on this very subject and what I found truly amazed me. You can't mention the colors of the rainbow without including the Bible, such as in Genesis, it is described as a sign of God's Mercy as well as the pact/covenant he made with Noah that such a flood would not be sent again. In Ezekiel, 1:26-28, colors of the rainbow are compared to the Glory of God, while in Revelation; Apostle John compares the rainbow colors to the Glory or Power of God, did anyone know this I surely didn't. So this makes me question why do people misuse His Holy Rainbow, why do they use it for their ill game or pleasure?

I recently asked my priest about His Holy Rainbow, such as the true colors and the true order of the colors and what does the order of the colors mean if anything? He never did give me an answer, is it because he had no idea? I think so if not then why didn't he answer me? Well in my recent research I discovered the order and it goes like this: ROYGBIV or starting from the bottom up VIBGYOR, which stands for Red Orange Yellow Green Blue Indigo and Violet. I must admit even after I found this research I still wasn't sure if these were the true orders or colors of His Holy Rainbow until the Lord Himself shined a rainbow into my living room and He kept it there until I counted the colors and the pattern of them and to my amazement it is all true, my true shame is rainbows are always shining in my living room even if there hasn't been any rain at all for some reason I just never paid attention to this Glorious Mystery until He asked me too, this is the true treasure at the end of the rainbow, not some pot of gold. I just wonder how many people really take the time to just reach out to the Lord and His Holy Rainbow just to say thanks.

I bet all of you want to know the true significance of the colors of the rainbow especially in modern philosophy. Can you believe it even in philosophy, a great deal of research has been done on this very subject in which I would of never known if God didn't ask me to write about His Holy Rainbow and the true importance of them, I can't thank Him enough for this honor, did you any of you know that colors play an important role in our lives? Different colors symbolize different personalities, and they even affect our moods differently, can you believe this? I couldn't until I really thought about it. The seven colors of the rainbow are also linked to chakra colors, seven days of the week, the colors of the Auras and so on. People even use crystals, did you even notice that when the crystals hit the sun just right all of the colors of the rainbow shine through. There are gems and other items in the seven colors of the rainbow that used for attaining spirituality, good health, and wisdom.

Let's revisit the seven true colors of His Holy Rainbow, and what each one represents: Red-this is the first color of the rainbow from the top it is also found in the ruby gem. Red signifies passion, vitality, enthusiasm, and security. It is also the light with the longest wavelength.

Orange-This light or color is a combination of yellow and red, which is also in a citrine gem, it is a dynamic color representing creativity, practicality, playfulness as well as equilibrium or control which I think we all can use a little of this.

Yellow-This is the color of the sunshine itself; the gem would be the yellow diamond. This color represents clarity of thought, wisdom, orderliness and energy. Let's face it we can all use this.

Green-This is the middle color of the rainbow and denotes fertility, growth, balance, health and wealth, the earth and the people have grown so much to the point that there is no more balance; the gem for this color would be the emerald.

Blue-This is the fifth color of the rainbow which makes us think of the unknown. The sky and the wide oceans are in this color and hence it has been associated with Spirituality and Divinity. What could be better? The gem for this color is a topaz.

Indigo-It is believed that this color of blue is calming, Indigo is sedating. Indigo is mystical as it bridges the gap between Finite and Infinite. Indigo colored gem stones are often used for spiritual attainment, psychic abilities, self-awareness and enhancement of Intuition, such as the sapphire.

Violet-The last color of the rainbow it is a mix of red and blue. It is considered the highest element of spirituality. It can ignite one's imagination and be an inspiration to artists. Dark tones of violet are associated with sorrow. A deeper shade of violet or purple denotes high spiritual mastery.

I think this holds true with the amethyst stone which has been known for its beauty and healing properties. The seven colors of His Holy Rainbow are not only a thing of great beauty but they also have

Biblical/philosophical significances, specific functions and purpose. Let me pose this question: Hasn't anybody realized that all of the colors of the rainbow are also all the colors of God's Green Earth, just look around just one day for no reason at all just stop look around and listen to all His colorful sounds. These are all the true treasures found at the end of His Holy Rainbow.

After doing all of this glorious research for the Lord I also realized that everything has a color and it comes in seven such as the teachings of Noah to mankind The Seven Basic rules to adhere to conforming to the Seven Colors of the Rainbow:

Thou shall not worship Idols
Thou shall not blaspheme
Thou shall not murder
Thou shall not have immoral relationships
Thou shall not steal
Thou shall Respect all Living Creatures
Thou Shall Set up Courts of Law

I wonder how many people can be accused of following these rules to the strictness of their intention. These are termed as: the Noahide laws- the Laws of Noah and the seven colors of the rainbow remind us of our obligation to them but how many really fulfill these obligations to our Lord?

Another important term related to the colors of the rainbow is the Angel Colors. I know, I was shocked by this information, I had no idea about colors of the Angels, but Devout Christians use these to focus on their Prayers to the Lord. Like the seven rainbow colors, there are seven Angel colors. Some gifted people with "sight" do not just see refracted light in the rainbow colors but another metaphysical system in which they believe to be Angels sent to Earth to guide us. These Seven Angel colors include:

Blue-Angel Michael (the leader of all angels). Also denotes Spirituality
Yellow-Angel Joseph (Thoughts/Wisdom)
Pink-Angel Chamuel-(relationships)
White-Angel Gabriel (revelation)
Green-Angel Raphael (healing)
Red- Angel Uriel (wisdom/energy)
Purple- Angel Zadkeil (angel of mercy).

After learning all of this information on all the wonders and beauty of God and His many Mysteries, how can anyone not want to love, adore, or be His servant and a witness to all of this that is a part of His church? Why do people not want to be a part of all of this? I don't know about any of you all but I will pray for you as I chase His Holy Rainbow. I pray that I will always be chasing His Holy Rainbow. After learning about His Holy Rainbow doesn't this give you the feeling to look at a rainbow and say to the Lord have mercy on me Lord and to pledge your life to Him?

I'M THANKFUL FOR

BY BERNADINE ZIEGLER
(11-25-07)

I'm thankful for the moon and the stars, without them I wouldn't know where we are, near nor far, can't you see how beautiful they are? I'm thankful for the air we breathe. Without it I couldn't even sing Alleluia.

I'm thankful for so many special things: such as my husband, my wedding, especially that because Jesus just didn't arrange the wedding he gave me such a perfect day, and families. God and his angels weren't just witnesses to my wedding, it meant everything to me, and of course my diamond ring.

I'm thankful for my health, although I did try to end it without God's permission. I almost destroyed his mission, that I'm not thankful for, but that is why I will give my admission to what I did, but he still saved me and that I will always be grateful for and so much more, I'm thankful for His Rain to ease and wash away my pain. Please God, don't stop the rain.

I'm grateful for my family because without them I wouldn't be crazy and free, I wouldn't be me, but most of all my granny Marie she is and always will be so special to me, I miss her, she was willing to give up her life for mine she loved her church and I as much I love and owe her so much.

I'm thankful for my skills of baking, and cooking, with these skills I can make anything, and I'm grateful for the food I receive from God, so I can prepare it for my husband's bounty, most of all the many gifts and many blessings from our lord whom I humbly thank and adore, to you I can't say much more, except for I Love You.

I'm thankful for the season for many reasons, but most of all snow time, especially in December, all that snow fun, and the blessed birth of God's Holy Son. Christ is his name and the Mass is his fame, equals CHRIST-MAS.

I'm thankful for the little children, how they just play the day away, I could just watch them the whole day, I'm grateful for his many critters and creatures and their innocence, watching them all day romp and play or maybe take a rest, and oh this is such joy for me. I'm thankful for all of God's living things such as the waterfalls, and the flowers in the yard or nature in its serenity, it's so peaceful in it's simple beauty and the smells so fresh and clean, God has been so good to me, I will always be thankful to thee.

IN THE NAME OF

BY BERNADINE ZIEGLER

(3-5-13)

In the name of the Father and Son, to whom do we speak about when you hear or say these words, do you really mean them? Do you really feel them? What is there true meaning? Do you really want to understand? Well I'll tell you, God is the Ultimate Father, His Son came down as man, His Name is Jesus, when He died on the Blessed Cross for us He became the Holy Spirit, Amen. Is this the reason why men beam with pride, Is this the reason why men are asked is it a girl or a boy? Oh the joy for the boy! Oh the sighs and cries if it's a girl.

Yes! We all have earth fathers to raise us and take care of us, I guess this is the reason why men always want to have a boy, why do the girls miss out, let's not forget about the Lord's Holy Mother Mary, She was once someone's daughter, without Her, ask yourself this: would you ever get to see God, or get to be with the Lord? Would we even have a world? I know nature would not be unfurled.

So I ask again why are the girls being denied? Why aren't the fathers beaming with pride when they have a daughter? Raising all of God's children is a gift that should never even be denied, they are not a death sentence. Ask yourself this: how did you get here and who raised you? Were you denied whether you are a female or male?

Just remember your mother came from somewhere and the things she had to bear do you really care? Always give praise to the Holy Mother and all she did for God and Jesus, to be a man you raise a daughter with all you can oh! How she will teach you how to be a real man, if you still can't understand or you don't want to be a man, then all I can say is just wait for God's trials for you, believe me you will be forever blue, or are you all in denial?

For all of the fathers on earth, just remember who created all of us no matter boy or girl, who carried you for nine months in the womb not a male, who nurtured you? You know it wasn't a male either, you should always thank the Lord above for his trust in you to raise his many blessed gifts, just like St. Joseph, who else was willing to raise the chosen one? God's Son. God loves us all no matter great or small, boy or girl, we are all part of our Creator there is no other.

To all fathers who raise or take care of us with God's guidance, and trust, just remember this who died on that Cross for us, the next time you hear or say those words while doing the sign of the cross, In the Name of the Father, Son, Holy spirit, Amen, do you really understand what those words really do mean?

Do you think you can do the same, do you know how to be, or what really makes you a man? Do you have what it takes to make you a real man, just like the Great I Am? He and loving His Mother is what it takes to make all of us, do your best to understand. We must stand and say these words, Lord I understand you are my Holy Father; Mary is the Holy Mother of Jesus, who is your Holy Son, by His Death He became the Holy Spirit, Amen. Now you are as one.

When are all of you going to understand? When we are mad at our fathers who mold and teach us, he will lead you, by the way God treats us, he is your Father don't make a stand he is just a man remember this most importantly, before you go cursing, yelling and shunning God out of your life, Just know that he is a Father too. He is The Most High Holy Father of us all. Without Him you wouldn't be you and nothing else would be true, you will surely take a great fall, you really have no choice. Hear and obey voice of choice.

LOOKING THROUGH ALL MY WINDOWS

BY BERNADINE ZIEGLER
(6/1/13)

Looking through all my windows. Sometimes I can do this all day, just watching the Lords' work at play; it helps chase my blues and cares away.

I wonder sometimes, why can't people just slow down and just look around? Why can't they see God's simple beauty and tranquility? It's very soothing to me. There are times when I look out my windows and think for long periods of time; it is funny when you look at something for a long time: and for some reason you just don't see it.

I have many windows: thirty one in all. In one direction I can see the critters at play and in the rear window I can see the leaves blowing, where are they going? What are we all doing? Why can't we just all stop and check this all out? When you look in someone's window you want to know what are they doing? Who are they? Do they see me? Why don't they invite me in, could they be a foe or friend, is there really somebody in there?

I recommend you look into your own windows and become your own judge. It is easy to look out a window and judge people, but what about when you're the one on the outside looking in? Then you become judged. How does this feel? Do you have a friend in the world who is really your friend?

Do you remember when your grandparents, and parents always said treat others as you expect to be treated, why don't we actually do this?

He is always there: His love, Forgiveness, Mercy, and Guidance is beyond compare. But without it really, where are you all going but in the land of nowhere? Think about it, when you look out or in any of your windows.

Instead of looking out your window and being the judge of something or someone I say stop for a minute and think: what if I become the judged one, would your world become all undone, can you finally realize it is no fun to be the judged one or the accuser, just stop and think I have been doing this all wrong, how can I fix this, what can I do? Don't forget you still have a friend: He sees and loves you no matter what you say or do.

Why doesn't everybody just open up all your windows and feel His breeze, just like a gentle touch on your face or just watch His Creation in its simple Serenity, why can't you open up your doors even if he isn't knocking and say to Him please come to me Lord please knock on my door, Lord please come to my window, what a wonderful sight that would be, so why can't we all just open up our windows, open up our doors for the Lord and say: I love you, I need you, please hear me, please come to me Lord, without Him who, where, and what are we really?

LOVE IS…

BY BERNADINE MISURA

Love is: here and ever after, tears and a lot of laughter,
When you get your first kiss from a fellow and you
hear the bells ringing, birds singing, the stars shining.
And you see the stars a shining all around, it feels like
a circle of angels, singing to you a beautiful love tune
from Above or the wonderful feeling of seeing God's
White Dove fly over you from the mountains view.
This is how you know you are in love.

Love is: what makes you happy even when you're with
your family, love is a beautiful thing even if you
don't receive the diamond ring, just search your
feelings then you will know that you're ready to let
your love grow and over flow so I say just let it
show for all to know.

Love is: when your partner in life asks you to become
husband or wife, love is also when you're in your
new house and you make a family with your spouse,
Oh! Yes you're in love.

Just when things start to look real bad: just remember
The special moments with your loved one that made
you happy and glad, love can do some amazing things
like wash away all your pain and the sun will dry up
all your rain, that's what love is.

But most of all: don't forget love is when there are no regrets, if you do however feel some regret just think of the first day you two met, I know you could never forget that happy day, perfect in every way. That's what love is about staying together and working things out. Love is also sent to you from God Above to catch you when you fall please do remember that God's love is Forever and ever after all.

MY GOD BOX

BY BERNADINE ZIEGLER
(4/20/15)

My God Box, you are probably wondering, what is a God Box? What do you do with it? How do you use it? What is it used for? What does a God Box look like? By all these questions you would think it is all a big loss. You give up wondering so you tuck this thought away, save it for another day, way far into the future; too far to mention. How do I answer, what do I say? All I can say is someday I would like to own one to find out all of the answers to all of these questions, But how does one acquire a God Box? Where does one go? Will no one show me, tell me someone please, sadly the answer is no!

As time went by, somehow, I did just tuck this thought away for another day. The thought really did go away, although at times, I did ask around and in return all I got was strange looks and frowns. I guess I just gave up, I would never find out and I would never find one in my life. Now too much time has gone by. Oh! Why do I even try? However, I did I still tried to find the answer to all my solutions, but really what are the questions? Then a miracle happened to me: I got married and my husband said to me, I have a God Box. I was in shock, how could this be, how did he get one, where did he get it?

I asked him all of these questions; he just simply answered me by saying, I have no idea! I have no answers, somehow it just got put into his stuff, and he didn't know what to do with it or what it is supposed to be used for. He said, when I get all my stuff, I will give it to you because I love you. I just thought to myself, how could this be that this man I barely know would give me such a gift, does he really know what this means to me? It is all a wonderful great mystery to me. I am filled with glee!

Someday soon I will get to see this box that has been haunting my deep memory.

The day finally came. I had the feeling of I can't wait but I will quietly wait Oh! The intensity Oh! What is the matter with me, why do I want this box so much? I did hear or read along the way in my life time the God Box was like mailing a Letter to God but for some reason I just couldn't believe this. How does one really send Him a letter, will He really receive it, will He really read it, how will He read it isn't Hebrew? I know He is the Creator of all but why would my inquiries matter to Him? Who am I to Him really? Will He answer me, Will He hear my plea? Oh! Woe is me.

My husband handed it to me and said there you are the box of your memories. He asked me do you know what it is for; do you know how to use it? I answered Yes Dear! I read somewhere it is like a mail box, you send Him a letter it is like getting a message to our Lord, he asked is that true, does that really work? I just couldn't stop looking at the box in my hand and then finally smiled at my husband and said, I don't know but I will love to find out. I placed it on my dresser I just couldn't stop looking at it.

It is really no different in its looks compared to a trinket box. It is even about the same in size, I opened it up and I saw a beam of white light how can this be what does this mean? It looks just like any other kind of trinket box, it has a prayer in it but everything else seems the same. Is this a letdown? But for some reason, I do not have a frown. Did I waste my time for some reason? I just don't think so: it took some time but I did finally decide to give it a try, but will He answer, will He really take my burdens and cares away that weigh me down with such pain and despair. I pleaded God help me, please.

I did write the Lord a Note, you ask what was on the note, just one of my many worries that I just don't want to carry anymore. So I opened the door to my God Box placed the letter in. I prayed to God and I closed the door, but to what do I have in store? All I know is that worry I do not have any more. I just opened up a door to a Heavenly World of so much more, which is what a God Box is: it is really a way to get a quick message to our Lord God Almighty; just like a mail box maybe it should be called God's Mailbox.

MY HOLY ROBED HEROES

BY BERNADINE ZIEGLER
(2-16-13)

My Holy Robed Heroes, What are they? Who are they? How many are there? These are all good questions but there are so many of these men to mention, but I'll give it a good try. These men all work for the Prince of Peace, The God of Love, and the One who Watches all of us from Above. Yes! All of them are priests, and so much more, such as they are not just there to save our souls by absolving us from our sins: they also double as my Marriage Counselors, My Therapists, My Teachers, and even My Friends in Christ, but do any of you ever really care or understand this kind of man?

Some of my Holy Robed Heroes, are from the past such as to name one, St. Francis De Sales, my Church is named after him, I really wish we could have met, what his letters did for people is unbelievable to me, and with his last breath of life he wrote a letter to soothe an old ladies pain of losing her husband, to me that is just amazing. What about St. Patrick, he has done so many things for others, but his biggest is saving the Irish from the pagans, to destroy evils reign. There are so many more, but these two I most adore.

My more recent past Holy Robed Heroes, I have met for a short time such as Father Flood, he was fun to see and talk to at Easter Penance Time. How about Father Stein, he didn't just answer my questions he brought me back to Gods Holy Church, he gave back my faith. He used objects in his homilies, not to put on a show but to get into the parishioners' mind and make everyone understand Love and Obey the Holy Words of the Great I Am, with Jesus and Fr. Stein, how could you not have a good time?

How about Father Schleicher, the Late Pastor of my Church, In confirmation class he removed evil from within me with a cup of water in a glass, how did he know? Did evil show? As teachers go, I can only think of one better and his name is Jesus, of course, who else? This is One Man we all should get to know.

There are others such as Father Zeisig, Oh! How funny you were, and Father Donnelly, people came to me and told me they hate you! I asked what for? They answered because he is very strict, and what I said to that, it's about time that a priest will follow the Holy Words and putting sinners in line. I also said he's English and his speech slips. Because he was born with too much tongue, believe me that isn't any fun,

And Father Byrider, after all you did marry my parents, even though you were in such pain, you never forgot. Even though we all just briefly met, the things these great men taught to me I will never forget.

Let's not forget the Holy Pontiffs such as Pope John Paul II; to him I say I am one of your biggest fans. I would have loved to just shake his hand or be married by him that would have been such a dream, and how he traveled around the world to save other sinners from their despair when people just didn't care.

He can't be beat, and the now leaving Pope Benedict XVI, he had a lot to clean up in His Holy Church, he made a vow if I don't feel well enough to attend to God's Holy Work, I won't leave anybody in a lurch, when he admitted he was feeling too weak to carry on the job he stepped down off of St. Peter's Holy Throne. Besides God, and Jesus, I think this is one of the most amazing men of all.

Then of course came Father Bline, Hey! What can I say? You are one of a kind, you are the most special to me even though my husband and

I came back after your arrival, God Told me to seek you out, and I said may I ask why? What is he all about? He answered I want you to be at his side, I said Yes! Of course Lord, anything You Ask of me.

He also said you and my priest have work to do for Thee. You are always there with a smile that beams for miles and miles, God is Looking at you and smiling too. I'd like to think that we will always be Friends in Christ if you don't mind. I thank God every day that you get to stay and save the Church I call mine, to stop it from following the wrong path, from satans evil wrath.

As for Father Suso, I will be sorry to see you go, on my Wedding Anniversary, as for us being Friends in Christ, that will always remain, but little did you know you taught me it's okay to be a little needy, weak, and childlike again but without all the pain, soon you will go to wash away other parishioners evil stains. I know God's Church is safely in your hands, I guess all I can say to you is God Bless You, and thank you.

All of these men are very special to me and will always be known as My Holy Robed Heroes. With all of these men as my Pastors and Priests, I will never be able to compete, they are all wonderfully unique, but being around some of God's Holy Vessels is and always will be such a real treat because they are also very sweet. When I am with one or more of them in God's House I always feel relaxed and at peace.

We all should get to Know and Love God and our Priests. God's Holy Chosen Vessels, they are here for all of us, to love and guide us, they all are and should be called our Holy Robed Heroes.

MY INSPIRATION

BY BERNADINE MISURA
(9-24-06)

This is for the two guys in my life whom I love, and adore, the first one always comes first; he is the greatest of all: the Good Lord Above. He has given me so much, such as His Forgiveness, his Guidance, His courage to help me through all my trials and tribulations in my life, He has also given me many gifts and blessings, such as His Immeasurable Love for which I am unworthy.

I will forever be in debt to him, but He still loves me even with my many frustrations in all situations, with His grace He always gets me through no matter what I do, for this I thank you and to let Him know He is my Inspiration. You have my Eternal Devotion.

My second is my soon to be husband, he is my white knight who kept calling me in the night, I don't know what it is you do for me, I guess it's your love unconditionally, it helps me with my procrastination, that slows me down.

For some reason while you're around, I feel I can do anything, I want you to know you are my everything, you are my gift from God, the only thing I can give you is my Eternal gratitude and my Eternal love. The both of you will always be in my heart forever, never to part, that I will carry with me every day; you are now and always will be my Inspiration.

A LETTER TO YOU

BY BERNADINE ZIEGLER
(1-28-11)

This is a letter to myself and anyone who knows what I go through, with no disrespect to you, I know whatever you must do for money to keep your family and business a float, I for one, don't want to rock the boat, I'm dirt water poor, and I will always be, I have no money I know it's not funny, I know you feel it too, don't feel so blue. It will be okay.

Someone asked me to tell them my favorite poets, how do I choose? I really don't have much to lose, I read a lot of old poetry, I was going through them all, I said, someday this could be me, then I asked myself, how could this be me? I'm not as good as them, and I may never be, unless God wills it of me.

If I must choose a poet: I would have to say Robert and Elizabeth Browning, and I'm a big fan of Edgar Allen Poe. I really understand and can relate to this man, because of reasons you may never know, you don't need to, it's Poe. I even enjoy T.S. Elliot.

I am a Native American, I have acquired some early Native American written works such as prayers and poetry, when I started to read them, I for some reason can't seem to put down my pen, I ask myself, is this the poet from within? I'll do as God asks of me, will you?

I hope so, this is my letter to you who do the things you must do to make it through, this is my letter of testimony, do what is right from inside. You know what you must do, this letter is tried and true, and May God Bless all of you.

MY LOST BROKEN ROSARY

BY BERNADINE ZIEGLER
(11/27/14)

My lost rosary: it was taken from me during a time when I was feeling lost in my religion, it was the last thing my grandmother touched, it was purple and white just like the colors for my school, it wasn't much, it was made of plastic beads, I had it blessed. When it was taken from me, I just couldn't cry, I felt so cold inside, I felt like I died. I think about it often, I know I will never see my old friend again.

I heard somewhere that if you take a blessed rosary from someone, you are doomed to go to hell. You would rather be in jail; unless you return it and ask for forgiveness by saying you are sorry. I don't know if this is true, if it is and I did this to someone, I wouldn't know what to do. I just want my old friend back, so I don't feel so blue.

I never learned how to pray the rosary. Every time I heard someone speak about it, I wanted to say, please show me, teach me, the words just never seem to come out of my mouth. For a long time I tried and tried to figure it out on my own, I felt so embarrassed that I am Roman Catholic and didn't know the rosary, so why is it important to me, why do I miss my old friend? I just wasn't sure. I just always felt like I had to hide from my own pride.

As I got older in life: I found out who and why the rosary was created, The creator is the Holy Mother Mary and why because it is a way to speak to Her Son through Her and the beads by saying the prayers: Our Father, Glory Be, and a lot of Hail Mary's, but I still didn't know how to use this information. Oh! My frustration and finding it hard to survive all my temptations.

After I got married: I finally figured it out, how everyone prays with the Holy Rosary, when I heard it at my church I said oh! That is how it is said, that is news to me, but is it really that easy? I still forgot how to say it all! Then the Good Lord called to me and showed me an easier way to say the Holy Rosary.

Now I don't need to hide, not even from Him, I wouldn't even try now, I don't feel so blue. And now I can say to the Holy Mother and Her Son thank you, now I know what to do.

Now I have a lot of rosaries, some broken and now repaired. You must never throw a rosary out, no matter what. Throwing out a broken rosary would be like throwing away a piece of our Lord, and he died on the Cross for you, no matter if we are in one piece or broken. I will always miss my old friend, now I have a rosary with me everywhere I go. All are blessed but a few and even the broken ones. So I say learn how to pray with your rosary each and every day, believe me your cares and many tears, will go away.

MY TIMES WITH GOD

BY BERNADINE ZIEGLER

(2/27/15)

Many of my visions that I have experienced over the years were when I still had my maiden name, some even when I was a kid. The majority was in the Clinton house. Well, during my years with epilepsy, I was having a battle with my body, every time my body had a seizure, I went up to Heaven to wait it out, and this went on for many years. I never told my family about any of this out of fear, many times I saw Angels, God's servants, and two other people, I went onto have many other visions: such as the day Gaby, my sister in-law, tried to kill me by driving she and I off an ice covered hilly road.

We did go off after I tried to get her to turn around before it was too late, as we went off a high ice cliff we were in the air for a while, I saw the hands of Angels holding the car. I felt them; there were at least three of them. They did put the car down after a while, when the angels did, Gaby asked me, did you feel that? I said what? After this, I have had a lot of moments with Jesus, and I always feel such great peace afterwards.

I must admit after I got out of the car, I walked back home. I didn't even check to see if she was alright. I didn't even check to see if I was alright. I just walked, I got into the house, and Mom was shocked to see me back. She asked, what are you doing home? I told her that Gaby tried to kill me, but I didn't tell her anything else.

My next vision did happen at my job Fussy Drycleaners, I don't remember any date, but the time was during the lunch break which was twelve in the afternoon, just about everyone was gone, it was two other workers and I in the back. Anyhow, I was filing clothes for the pressers, I saw this glow out by the presses, I had to see what it was, as I got closer, I noticed it was a man, he was in white but there was such a green glow around him, I got real close, I discovered it was the Lord Jesus. He said, My Child, come closer so I did, then He Said Bernadine come, I said, My Lord, at a bow I said, who is it you came to see? What is it you need of me?

Is it me you are looking for my Lord, please tell me? He Smiled at me and said, My Daughter, I Came for you! I was about to Kneel, He Said my name. Don't worry, I have work for you. I was shocked and I could not breathe, I finally said, My Lord, I am here for you, ask of me, what is your will? I must have had a tear in my eye because He Said, No Tears My Daughter! He Said I need your help! I said, your will is my will. Then He Stood up and went through the wall, the others came back from break, I told no one.

It took some time before I tucked those words away. My family and I were now moving to the Clinton house, I was driving there one day, and I heard my name, from where I didn't know. He said, You Look My Daughter! I said, my Lord, I'm driving, He Said, Look Up! So I did, it was a cloud of a Unicorn. I didn't know what that meant. I said, my Lord, that is a pretty cloud, but I do not understand the message, He said Look Up! So I looked again, it was an image of His beautiful Face, a Perfect image. I somehow drove up to the house safely, I parked, I looked up in the sky again, and I saw the cloud turn into the unicorn again, I didn't think about this again because I didn't understand any of this, I know I must ask a priest, and I finally asked my pastor, and he nearly fell out of his confessional chair. He knew the answer, and I understood a little more, I even relaxed a little bit more.

Some time went by at least a couple of years, then one night I was praying to God again, I fell asleep and for a while I felt a finger rub the palm of my hand. I didn't wake up at first, because I thought it was a dream. I felt it again but stronger; I woke up in a state of shock. I stood up against my bedroom wall for an hour, at least looking around for something or someone who woke me up, my door was still closed, I saw no one or nothing, so I slowly went back to bed, but no to sleep.

Just when I got more relaxed, I heard many voices, some were laughing and most of them were female, even the one that said, do you ever think she will figure it out?

I heard a lot of no's but the one male voice said, in time she will figure it all out! She will come around and understand and come to me, all of these voices were very clear. I heard many of them but after the male spoke, the others went away. I didn't know what to think about any of this, so I told no one ever. One other time my father noticed a very long cut on my arm. It must of happened while I was asleep I told him, because he asked me about it, I did say I didn't know when it happened or how. He said that is an awful large cut to not feel or know about it.

I looked down at it; it is in the shape of a lightning bolt.

I knew he was right, but I couldn't tell a soul. I prayed a lot and went to confession, even more I prayed. One time I prayed during the day and He answered me by sending a rainbow, but not an ordinary rainbow, this was many colors of grey and blacks. I thought to myself, as I looked at it but was this just really for me? Then my mother mentioned the next day about the odd rainbow she saw. I was amazed to hear someone else saw it. I even asked her, what you think this means? She said, I don't know, maybe nothing.

Maybe she is right, maybe she is wrong, I was always amazed at how odd things were done to me and have not known why, for instance I used to levitate for many years in my childhood, I always feared when it happened because I had no idea how why or who was doing this to me. I was always so tired afterwards, I was so afraid if it would happen in church and I would levitate and look at the priest in the eyes, Oh!

Imagine my embarrassment, in fact I'm not sure when it stopped, but I never had any experiences in the Clinton house, now I understand who was doing this to me and why, I also know why I wouldn't mind if it did come back. There were even times in the old Barberton house I walked through doors without moving them, that stopped early in my life, but it was still kind of cool. I mean, who else can walk through doors without opening them?

My father always told us kids about his times when he saw Angels, now I will never say he is telling stories, but I also had some experiences such as these and never told anyone for the reasons that they would say I was making up stories, so why bother? I thought to myself, and because if you even tried to over shadow my dad you would have received a whipping anyway, and I didn't need any of that. When my nephew was young, he always spoke of angels. We always asked him about them, but now he is grown up, and he has never spoke about them now. I often wonder why? Before we moved into the Clinton House, we had left our church because the wrongdoings the pastor was committing against the church. We just couldn't stay because of all the accidental deaths. I feared for my life and I guess my parents do too.

This I think was a miracle, not a vision; I was at my dry cleaning job. Ohio is suffering a mini-drought. People were starting to get worried, including my co-workers, the power went out for some reason, so we went outside, they were all off talking, I was looking up in the sky, and I was watching the clouds just for fun. I decided to motion my fingers to tell each cloud where they need to connect to another cloud to form a storm. As I kept doing this, the clouds really were going where I was telling them. Then the last cloud went into place, then a very strong storm, a thunder storm full of high winds, we went back inside because it was less safe for us to be outside.

But what I heard all day from these co-workers of mine that I created the storm. That I made the storm as powerful as it is because I am a Native American. I said to them, do you really think I have power as strong as God to make a storm like that? They all said yes! I shook my head and said; no way will I ever want that ability.

One other time many years after this incident. I was at my Canton house, Canton was suffering a slight drought like all of Ohio did many years earlier, it was very hot outside, people were suffering heat exhaustion, so I stood in my driveway, spoke to God and then I did a rain dance in my driveway until it started to rain, but this time, no one knew who was responsible for all the rain. I think it rained for three days, at least now I don't hear any drought talk, now were these miracles. I don't think so, I say these were Gifts from God: but I say let the people think it, God and I know better.

My first vision was in the new house in the nineties. In my vision, I was traveling. I think I was on a pilgrimage in Egypt and got lost, it was getting dark, I was walking through sand mounds and it was very hot. I was thirsty, hungry, and dirty, from the blowing sand, it is even getting in my eyes, then after a while I saw a light, it was in the distance but somehow I made it there. I knocked I waited for a while then I heard a noise the door opened, a woman answered, I told Her about my plight, and She let me in, She even gave me soup, She said Her Name is Mary. I heard a lot of people are named Mary in these parts, so I didn't think anything about that, She kept saying eat, eat, sit, so I did while Mary stayed busy around Her House.

The soup was tasty and it made me warm again, I was still eating it when Her Husband came in with a load of wood for the fire. Mary called out his name Joseph. She said, this is our guest, Bernadine. I turned around to say hello, but then I remembered I never told Her my name. Then I thought for a moment Joseph and Mary, I couldn't stop looking at them. Joseph said hello, I gestured a hello to him then I heard a Baby cry. Joseph said, Mary, the Baby. She went to go attend to the Baby, He came out: then I finally discovered who they are, to my embarrassment. This is the Holy Family.

I said it's Jesus, I went to my knees, I said, Holy Mother, forgive me. Saint Joseph, Please forgive me! Mary Smiled and said, this always happens to us, She Said, please get up, I bowed She asked, Do you want to hold Him? I couldn't breathe: I hold the Holy Baby, She walked towards me and placed the Baby in my arms, I still couldn't breathe. He was smiling and cooing to me, I smiled and whispered, Please forgive me, Lord. He continued to coo and smile at me; I still smile when I think about this moment. It's too bad I can't tell anyone, because they wouldn't hear me.

There was another unusual vision: this one kind of scared me, because I still don't know what this one meant, this very large man I saw in a black long trench coat, he was some distance from me. I saw he was carrying something, he got a little closer to where I could see, and he was carrying a dead person or a bad angel. The eyes of the being in his arms were somehow staring at me. The eyes are like black holes, the skin was dark but that is all I could see, then this very large figure just kept walking on, then this vision was gone.

Then we moved into the Clinton house, but didn't return to the church right away, all of these visions, I kept experiencing. When I did find a church to call my own, one of the first visions was when I was standing on a mountain because I was called by Him. I said, Lord I am here! He appeared in Green Attire, He was walking towards me with a cane, but He didn't need it. I saw the bright light of his Halo.

He didn't smile, so I was worried as He got close enough for me to hear Him. He Said I NEED YOU COMFIRMED NOW! I said, yes My Lord, I will do as you say. I had this experience while I was in church during a Sunday Mass. The feeling after I returned was great, the priest was saying the announcements for the day, and he said adult confirmation classes on Monday, the day after. All I could do was smile and said, you are good, you didn't even give me time to change my mind, and I heard Him laughing, and what can you do after that? But I do as He says, so I did and never looked back.

While taking the class I had another one, it was all the people in the class in a room. And our pastor arrived in a holy red robe and then he left the room for some reason, then the associate priest came in to take over, he also was in red. Again for some reason, I am the only one that sees this happening. Then the associate was called away, he was gone for a while. None of us knew if the class was over, but no one left either, so we waited then. Finally, the pastor came back in white, and so did the associate to tell us the class is over, and confirmation is in a couple of days. So what did that mean, not sure? I got confirmed and so did the others in the class. But maybe they didn't stay with the church as they promised, I don't know.

I am married now, and we had a true wedding in Holy Matrimony, while God's Wedding was being performed, I felt warm hands running up and down my left leg. I looked around and there was no one near me. I think it was God's Angels, I mean, after all, the most important witness to our wedding was and always will be the Lord God, but before the wedding the night before, He sent up many rainbows for us. They were all very beautiful. I'm guessing He accepts our wedding as His.

Every time I pray to Him, He hears me; He always gives me a token of some kind to tell me He is here, and that He heard me. He even taught me how to pray the Rosary the right way His Way, and every time I do, I always see a part of Heaven open up, and I have even seen faces of His Angels, it is an awesome feeling, but the visions never stopped and I pray they don't.

This vision happened when I was being cleared of the epilepsy, and the pills, it was in the year 01, when my new doctor asked me to get a M.R.I. When I was put into the testing tube for the scanning, I just was in a panic I kept praying to God, just before I was going to bang on the tube, I heard someone calling my name. I looked in front of me, there were two very large images standing in front of the wall. Their wing span is far and wide I couldn't count all the feathers, I heard the male voice say, and we need to calm her down. The Lord needs her to be still, then the female shouted no, don't move! Then she whispered, be still.

The male repeated the words at a whisper. I asked with my thoughts, Are you the Lords Highest angels? No answer, but their angels unfurled to show their length, then the female voice said, be still! You are almost done, and then the assistant running the test asked me questions to see if I was alright, and to tell me the test is done. I looked back to find that they were gone, but I will never forget this day, this is one of many miracles.

One of my visions in the year 2002, when I was praying to God like I always do, I was praying hard. I must have fallen asleep or gone into a trance of some kind, I think. So all I could see was a dark nearby place. And it is kind of foggy, and I am talking to some man, but I can't hear what he is saying. But I can see him perfectly: blond hair, bold green eyes, navy pants, and a camel color woolen trench coat, with black dress shoes. Just when I was about to figure out what he was saying, another man just walks through us like we are dead, or he is, and that is what he is trying to tell me.

All I could see was the back of his curly long brown hair, grey trench dressed very similar to the other man, all I could do was stand there and stare, I could not move. So I watched the grey trench coat as he kept walking by, I noticed one of his arms was cupped like he was carrying something, but I couldn't tell. I still can't see it is still foggy, and got thicker for a minute more. The fog cleared, I see what he has, and it is another man.

I see his face, but there are no eyes like they were taken out, I thought to myself, why am I seeing this before the grey trenched man got out of my sight? I called to the Lord, the man in the black trench coat, where did he go? No answer. This image went away then the colors I kept seeing were changing like the colors of the rainbow, until I woke up. I think I stayed awake for some time to keep praying, but couldn't help wondering who and where I was? Shortly after this, there were some glowing orbs in my bedroom, my cat even saw them and got very scared. I spoke some more prayers and told them to be gone, but I know that would be temporary, so I spoke to my priest, he said some prayer to bless the house and critters that live here and now thank God the orbs are gone.

Another vision is also in the year 02; I call this one the Angel: I was standing in the middle of nowhere, it seemed I looked around at my surroundings, and there is a man. I didn't say anything because I wanted to see what he is going to do at this distance, he probably wouldn't have heard me anyway. All I can tell is, he is bending down like he is looking down at the flowers, and he has a smile on his face like he has no care in the world. I just stood there; it seemed like for hours just watching him.

I kept thinking how beautiful he looked as I looked I wondered if he was an angel, then something must of startled him because he popped up his head, then my question was answered, his wings popped out then, also, he stared at me for a while, then he smiled. I just couldn't stop looking at his wings, he never said anything, but I think he was there to tell me God hears me. I should not worry; everything is going to be just fine. I still don't know which angel it was, then for some reason, the angel threw his arms up as to toss something in the sky towards Heaven, but all I can think of is: stones of jasper, sapphires, and tigers eye in a silver ring, just as he opened his hands, he turned, smiled then he was gone.

The next vision started by me standing in an unfamiliar place: I didn't know where or how I got here, so while standing in place, I looked around to see if I can see something familiar, no! I couldn't but I noticed there are no trees here but there is some vegetation but not a lot most of the surroundings are desert, there is some mountainous area; but it could be sand dunes off in the distance, the longer I looked around, the more I got confused, so I shouted out my question to God, why am I here, and where am I? No answer. So I continued trying to move so I could look around further, but no luck some time went by, it seemed like hours then suddenly there was a light breeze. Where is it coming from? I don't know, the breeze got stronger, the sands started to blow, the breeze got so strong to the point that I couldn't see any more. Then the breeze started to slow down.

I see a light shining brightly through the blowing sand and then the breeze just stopped. Then I saw a very tall image in the distance: it slowly started walking past me, it is now kind of dark out, I think it's night; but what I do see is a Man dressed in gray cloth or maybe a robe, but I don't think that is His real color. He is smiling, He seems happy about something. He looks like He's looking for something; for what, I am not sure. But for some reason, I can't stop watching him. I am still trying to move to call at Him to help me, but I just can't. The Man walks closer to the desert flowers; He bends down to pick one then He looks up like something startled Him.

Then He just started getting brighter like a light just turned on; to my shock, it's His Halo, it is so bright it could light up the world. Then he looked at me, and still smiling so bright for some reason. I feel so complete, but I don't know what to do or how to react, then He pretended to smell the flowers He already picked. He started to walk away, and then He called out my name and said, I am very pleased with you My Child! He went on to say, don't worry, you are loved! Then he walked on and I somehow ended up back in my room. I think this was God.

This vision, I call the light: one night I was praying as always to Lord Jesus, and His Holy Mother, I must have been praying for at least an hour and a half. *I had a lot of things to thank Him for and a lot of evil for Him to take away. Then I opened my eyes; I lay on my stack of pillows, so I could look at the stars outside, so I can fall asleep. Then it happened: this big beam of light came from a star off to the north, it was so bright it almost blinded me, but all I could do is watch it just like someone was giving me a message. It looks like the Star of David, or as I call it God's Star. But all I do know it is so beautiful, all I could think was, it's too bad I have no one to tell about this sight. Then I lay back down again, I asked God, was that for me, Lord? The beam of light on the star got brighter and whiter than before. It was more of a yellow color, and then I must have fallen asleep.*

The next set of visions are from the year 03: I can remember this very quick vision, I was falling asleep one night, and then I must have ended up in a different place. This place had a dark and lonely feeling, there is a man in black he is kind of far away, he is saying something, I can't make it out, and he looks very sweaty from all the steam and smoke all over the place. He as at a bend almost like he is steering something, while looking at me. This world is evil, dark and lonely. He is even wearing black, I feel so cold I decided I must leave this area; I said God, please take me away from here. And he did, because the guy in black got further away.

This vision I think about a lot is this one, it is also short: I was called to a forest, I was standing on a lovely stone bridge, everything looks so green, water looks blue, also that it's because of the reflections I just couldn't help but look around and in this place. I could move around, I just kept watching the water, it didn't move very fast, I was about to put my hand in the water, then I saw a Face. A Man's Face, He is smiling playfully, I looked to see where this man is. There is a Man right next to me; He bent down dipping His Hands in the water to cleanse His Face. He did this three times, He rose up and dropped the rest of the water in His hands, and then He said my name still playfully I didn't know what to do or say finally I said, my Lord, He Said you can call me J.C.

I haven't ever seen the Lord like this. He Said in a joyful voice, you're wondering why you are here? Before I said anything, He Said relax, calm down, I'm here! I didn't even realize I was uptight, but His Words really did give me peace, these words mean a lot to me because of my past, I so needed someone there who cared for me because I lost my granny, I miss her so and by His Grace He is still here for me.

This vision happened in the year 03: on New Year's Day, it was 4 in the morning. I wasn't sleepy or tired at all, everybody went to sleep. So I went to my bed to lie down, I closed my eyes to pray to our Lord. As I was praying, I think I fell into a deep meditation, because I don't think I was asleep. I ended up in this Egyptian building, it is beautiful, but where am I? I think I'm in Egypt, but I can't be sure anyway. I went to have a look around; I was walking for a while. It was a very good walk, I felt very refreshed, not tired at all. I saw a lovely large stream up ahead, so I stopped there to rinse the sand off of me.

I hear it itches if you leave it on for too long anyhow, as I bent down to get some water in my hands to rinse my face, I noticed it smells sweet, but I didn't get to taste it because I saw a Face coming up out of the water. Where is it coming from? There is no one around. It's a Man's Face and it's not happy looking, as I kept looking at him, I realized the Face belongs to Jesus. I smiled, and thought to myself, why is He Unhappy?

His Face was starting to disappear, so I decided to move further down the stream, I must have gone about a mile from where I was before. I stopped because I saw a glowing light. I had to see what it was, I am on top of a hill, I am looking over a cliff, but from a distance. I can see the light it is coming from down below. I thought to myself, do I go further, do I dare? The light came closer to my eyes, it is a Man, He is in White, and He is looking at the surroundings like He senses something or someone. He is smiling for some reason, can He Hear Me does He Know I am here? He turned around I could barely see him as he got closer I noticed who the man is. I whispered it's you Jesus Christ, I looked at Him, I asked Him through my thoughts, What do you ask of me Lord, He didn't Answer me.

After He didn't give an answer from the last vision, I must have fallen into another, because I hear voices, I arose from my bed and went running down the stairs to see who it is. I got to my living room and no one was there. So I went back to my bed. I clasped in bed like I was dead, then I went back into the vision where the Lord gave me no answer, I was back at the stream, the Man in White was standing there, His Back was turned and I wanted to touch his Hem of His Garments. The Garments of Jesus Christ, but for some reason, I did not maybe out of fear. I just spoke to Him instead through my thoughts; He turned and looked at me. He smiled, then He bent down to wash His Face, then the vision was gone! I heard the voices of my mom and sister, they came home from work. Then I heard the TV. Or I even hear the dogs barking, I didn't feel like I was asleep, but I dare not go down there, the next morning I felt refreshed even though I have had no sleep.

"The Burning Tree" is the next one: I was having trouble sleeping like always, I was lying in my bed counting the jets that went by. Some people count sheep, I count jets, because we live behind the airport. I don't know how long I was counting the jets coming and going as I was falling asleep. I kept staring at this very large tree in front of my house, I kept thinking if a bomb was dropped and it touched that tree, my house and the neighbor's house would go up in flames. As the image became clear, the vision was becoming more real.

I was trying to figure a way to put the burning tree out, before it did some major damage to both houses, as I was looking around for things to use, I discovered we still have a lot of snow. So I hurried and found a shovel, I kept shoveling like there was no tomorrow. There were a lot of people watching me, not lifting a finger to help, but when the tree stopped burning, they weren't laughing at me anymore. Then there was no more vision, what did it mean? I'm not sure.

At this point, I didn't have any visions for three years. But don't think for a moment God left me. He didn't, in fact; I spoke to Him a lot and He gave me little gifts to tell me, He heard me. This is still going on and always will be. I can remember one of God's messengers: it was a white moth, it was at night, and it was the start of fall season, because we had the house gas on in my new house, I opened the door and this white moth flew straight up into the sky. As far as I know, bugs don't do that, not even at night, and there were no lights on outside, just God's stars. But that isn't the only time I had with a bug, or even a white moth, there was one other time I was cleaning the walls...

I saw a big white glop on the wall; I thought it was just a glop of paint. Then I got my flyswatter to use a scraper, I placed it by the glop of paint and it moved. I jumped, then I moved the swatter closer, so the white bug could get on it safely, so I could put it outside, and it did and so did I. I have rescued many bugs after these moments, like a very large dragonfly from a cruise ship. I was the only one who could see it, and I got it on a newspaper somehow, and then let it out a window on the ship, it was suffocating from no air. And two other moments in my life. I rescued about four dragonflies from being crushed into the soil. I placed them on the leaves nearby, until they got air back into their lungs, come back to me in spring to say hello, we're back.

There have also been times with the birds such as a pair of hoot owls: I was taking out the trash in the morning, and I saw the owls hooting to each other, we must get to the nest. I just said in the speech, can I see you two first before you go home to your nest? And then somehow, I ended up with two beautiful birds on my arms, one on each. Then I spoke, are you two my hooting friends? Then they both hooted at the same time to answer me. I said, thank you my friends, for stopping in! Now you must get to your nests! They flew up into the sky, tapped beaks, and then they flew in different directions. I was truly amazed by this, and then a few months later, I was outside feeding the birds, when I finished with the seed.

I was standing still, I saw this very large bird coming my way, I didn't have time to move, I put my arm up, then this large bird landed on my arm. I was so amazed but petrified at the same time, I spoke to the falcon. I said, you are beautiful, but why did you grace me by landing on my arm? All I heard from my mother was, don't move! she wanted to get a picture because she didn't believe this was happening to me, I guess when I was younger, I could always speak to the wild critters. But I never knew why or how, but at this moment I did finally enjoy it. There was one final time talking to the birds, I can remember, it was a silly one. I was reading in the sunlight on a very warm summer day. This small red capped bird walks over towards me, looks up at me, flicks its wings at me, cheeps loudly, motions it head towards the bird seed house to tell me hey! we need seed! Hey! I am hungry, feed me now! I said out loud oh!

Is that right? It cheeped at me again. I said, alright bossy! It cheeped at me again, watched everything I did, waited for me to finish, when I left it went to the seed house. I said, is there enough for you? You know it looked at me, went to pick up some seed, cheeped at me, and then it flew to its nest to tell its mate, okay! There is more seed. I just shook my head, then smiled and went back to my book. Until I saw its mate come to the feeder, then cheeped to me to say thank you, human. I bowed to her, and said, you are welcome my lady bird. I still think of these moments every day because this was all caused by a dog bite I received when I was 13 years of age. Ever since I have had a better communication skill to speak the wild.

In fact; I can remember a time when I was in church, I was listening to my priest Fr. Bline on the altar, and then I saw some angels pass by me one by one. It was very clear that Seraphon, the first female looking angel, she spoke to me and asked to tell my priest that she is pleased with him and why, another example: My previous pastor passed away and two days afterwards I saw him as clear as day light. He was in white, and he was at the Tabernacle trying to figure out how to open it. He gave up, kneeled, and went into the back of the church; I guess to move on.

Here's another moment: It was during Advent, I think the Tabernacle was wide open all through the Mass, which I thought was odd in itself. I just couldn't stop looking at the Incased Host sitting in the Tabernacle. I saw it slowly rise, and it did this more than twice during the mass, I was not sure if anyone else saw this phenomenon, but I dare not tell the people next to me in the back of the church after the mass. I told my priest about it, for some reason, he wasn't surprised, before I could ask him, why? He told me, he has seen this happen also, you couldn't imagine my relief when I heard this, I always thought I was seeing things, crazy something along that line.

Another moment: I again was in church, I saw Jesus Christ, He even said Hi! He sat down in front of the church, in the pews across from me. He came to see Fr. Bline become the pastor to His church and one final moment like this is: when I heard the Voice of Jesus Say to me that He doesn't like the way people are mocking His priest by the way of using their hand motion during the Our Father prayer in the mass. in fact; He sounded quite angry.

One final thing: there was one time when my new pastor was away on vacation, and I saw the candles lit before the beginning of the mass, one was leaning oddly and all I can see is my church burning away while my pastor is gone out of country. I told him about it when he came back, but at times they still light them before mass. I have had many other visions and moments of hearing His Voice, but I put them to some of poems or short story.

I can remember one time in the morning I was going to work, and I saw a dark cross image on the back of a large truck right in the middle of the back end, I followed all the way to work. Another time when one of my friends from church died. I prayed for her and then next day I saw three crosses in the sky just like the crosses on the mountain where Christ was crucified, one other moment I saw two rainbows in the sky, one of them was broken but they were large and beautiful.

This one was so real: it was when I was dating and I wasn't sure if this was the one I should marry, I asked God and Jesus to appear on the hotel wall? my date didn't notice, but I heard the Lord say no! Then He motioned His finger toward my date and he grew two horns, I was shocked by what I saw, the man I was with kept talking about how I was going to have sex with him without a ring, he said you had better hurry and find a husband before I can't have kids. I was so mad! I just said, take me to my car so I can go home, he went to pay the bill in the hotel lobby, and I saw the image of the Holy Family on a vending machine as clear as day. And to my surprise, he came out and asked me if I saw the image I said no! I did, but I lied to him, I saw it, I just wanted him to learn to not try and rape a woman anymore and he tried several times with me, and by God's Will I got through.

This one I called The Dead: it happened in the 2010, it is a normal night for me, I going to pray to God before I go to sleep like always, then all of a sudden, I find that I am in some kind of open room. I'm not sure of its location, it could be in the sky or someplace else, but it is very open and there are brown rocks all around, there is a person here, it's a man and he has some blue on him and some white. I am not sure if this is an angel or man. Wait a moment, he is saying something: it sounds like I must go! Then he was gone.

Now I see a woman floating in the air, her hair is red and she has blue eyes, she is standing in mid-air so it looked, for some reason I said, Judy go home to the light! Although I have no idea who this lady is or what she is. Then another lady appeared. She looks like someone I know, but I know it isn't here. So I called out, called out the name Joan, for some reason she is at a squat or a sitting pose in mid-air.

I said, Joan go home to the light of God! She is crying, she came closer to me, it really does look like my friend, Bonnie, I said as she was crying, she got quiet and nervous, but still crying; I said I know, I love you, too. But you must go to Him, He's calling you home. It will be okay, you will be fine! Then I felt some warm hands, about four in reality rub my arms. I touched my arms and they are more warm then the rest of me.

The three images of Christ, the first one was a beautiful iron arch display with Christ in the middle, and He is so Happy and all around the arch are white flowers, they are so beautiful, I know why He sent this to me, I was praying to Him and this is the way He answered me. The second one is very similar to the first one, but He wasn't in the middle like the first. I said out loud, those flowers are beautiful! I wonder what they are? He answered Morning Glory. The third image was a very large Cross with Christ in the middle, but all the images were made from iron in an arch display and they are all very beautiful, I woke up very refreshed, rested, and happy. Thank you, Jesus.

This is called rosary 3, I am not sure if this was a dream or vision, I was in the pew right next to the choir singing during the mass, I was looking down from the top of the church at this lovely large hanging pink rosary, as for the rest of the church, I noticed the rosary was dangling, but ever so slightly, it is a soft clear pink color and a silver background, and the church also has some pink from within. With stone white all about the church, it is just beautiful. I don't remember a priest being there or a mass being performed, but for some reason, there are a lot of people and what are they waiting for, I am not sure. I am waiting for my husband, while I was waiting, I just couldn't stop watching the rosary.

Something made me think of the two white rosaries I have. Then I heard a voice next to me, it is my husband and he sat down next to me. I smiled at him after he sat down. I asked him to look at the rosary on the wall see how it is dangling, we both kept watching it, and he finally said how is it doing that? There are no windows and the doors are closed. Then I saw a holy man. I couldn't see his face, but I did see him reach for the hanging rosary, how did he get that down, it was hanging higher than his reach.

All the other folks didn't see him, and then I saw what was wrapped around his arm. There are two other rosaries, they are white and I got a good look at them. They are my white rosaries, the large pink rosary from the wall he placed with the other rosaries, and then he walked away. I kept thinking who is it what's his name? Then I realized that my husband and I are in the front pews, and we weren't before. Then I got a closer look at the holy man. But only his back side, I never got to see his face, he is in white and his hair is brown to black color. I kept thinking, how does he know we are here? I wanted him to turn around; I did finally see his profile before he went away. He looks like my husband but taller and longer in body, then he went away.

These two visions were back to back: and probably my strongest and the more clearer ones. I woke in a cold sweat from both of them; I have had these visions quite often. the first one I call His Holy Scepter: I went to a church and I usually am frequent in the vision, I went to sit down in a chair in the middle of the church, the mass was about to start so I was going to turn off my cell phone, but God said no! Turn on my

Holy music. There is no one to sing for the church or the mass. So I did, I programmed my phone to play church music. The priest was coming, I heard it was a new priest so I had to see who it is, and as he got closer I couldn't help thinking he looks familiar. For some reason, I have seen priests with canes but this one has something golden. What is it? I couldn't help thinking and what is he going to do with it in the mass?

He is dressed in all white vestments, as he got on stage, there was no altar in this part of the church, and the people were getting louder than the priest, so I told them to be quiet so I can hear what he is saying. I heard him going on about evil and how not welcome it into your life and how to destroy it when it tries, I finally found out what the golden staff is. A golden scepter and when the priest bent it down, it lit up with this powerful light stronger than lightning. He shined this light on a couple of people who were on the stage with him; they are dressed like nuns but are they really nuns? They just disappeared like they weren't even there. As he went on, I discovered who he reminds me of, it's my priest! Why is he in this vision? he saw me and stared at me, could he possibly know me, how could he know?

Does he really remember me in this vision? He pointed the scepter towards me I thought he was going to destroy me and calling me evil how could he think that? I love the Almighty and my priest. He shouted out the words, evil be gone away with you! Then the light came out and split apart, and zapped the two people on both sides of me. I couldn't stop screaming, then the priest went on to explain more about how to evaporate evils lure, why we must repent and stand up for God and His Laws, he used the scepter one more time in the audience. People were screaming and running out of there.

As the folks were leaving, I went to speak to the priest, I asked him do you know who I am, and do you remember me? Through my thoughts he didn't answer, but he looked straight at me, I can't help but think how much he looks and sounds just like Father B, my pastor. My phone was playing Holy music the song was "Jesus, We Didn't Know

It Was You" I thought this was odd. He looked around for it, but before he picked it up and handed it to me. He commanded that everyone sing along with me, but there was just about no one left, he motioned his hands towards me to hand me the phone.

We sat down next to each other but he wasn't happy at all, the people were still screaming and running they are trying to get out of the church, but they weren't successful. He locked the doors before he started preaching. When he arose from his seat next to me, and he said those Holy Words. All I could say was thank God, and I continued to pray, then I woke up in a cold sweat.

This one really scared the death out of me: I was called to this very old church, its location I don't know, I was blind folded. I was told to go to an old office, I already had my blindfold off, so I looked around the room, it's dark and everything is made from white stone. I wasn't alone for long, This man came in, he is in all black he is of grandpa age, and without my knowledge there was more than one man all in black in the room. The older one told me to kneel, I didn't have time to say anything, and another man got behind me to hit me in the back of the knees to force me to kneel on command.

I fell forward, my hands landed on this picture. I think a painting hit me in my face as well, the picture moved when I landed on it. There are three images, all three have a yellow glow around their heads like halos, and I was a little shook up still. Then I heard one of the men say, do you yield? Before I could answer they also said, do you love Him, will you obey Him? Then I heard the words, do you yield? But more forceful and louder, I got down further onto the image of the Holy People I begged for mercy. I continued to say, Lord I am yours and always will be. Mercy, Lord have pity on me. Do with me what you will. I'm unworthy Lord have mercy on me. My soul, my life's blood. Everything is yours Lord. I kissed the images on the floor. I got up even out of fear of being beaten again. When I did get up, my wrists are in terrible pain, then I woke up in a cold sweat! I was nervous for days, the following week the same picture was on my church bulletin. I so wanted to tell my priest about this, but for some reason, I never did.

This one, the year 2014: I still can't believe this one. I took a morning shower, and then I came down stairs to exercise when I was done. My dog Oscar discovered blood on three of my toes on my right foot, where did it come from? I don't feel any pain. I checked to see if I am injured but I am not, not anywhere. Then I checked all of my critters to see if they are bleeding, and there is nothing I can find. I am thinking this is God's doing, but what did I do to earn this gift? Is this part of the stigmata? If so, then I really am honored, but still not sure why or what I should feel or do. I don't know what to say or if I can even tell my priest what will he think, will he believe me? I must admit my foot did feel different it still does at times; it makes me feel nervous because my dog kept sniffing my foot that night.

This one took me a while to understand, but I did get the answer. This one started with me looking in the mirror, and somebody behind me kept putting white feathers in my head, not in my hair. But in my head, a total of 8 in all, but who was adding these feathers and why, I did continue to talk to the voice or person, I will probably never find out who is putting the feathers in my head, but I did find the answer to this vision. The white feathers are rewards because of the people I helped come back to Christ and the church and when I am called Home to God, the formation of the feathers are to be crowned in heaven. I did tell my pastor about the feather vision, he seemed most curious but he had no answer. But he said, I pray you do find the answer and just a few days later I did, but I never did tell my pastor the answer.

I did have another vision: I was dressed in nun attire. I said in shock, I'm a sister? I must admit I didn't believe that I'm a nun, how can this be? But I did play with the clothes by rubbing the white cloth to my face, but, how can I be a nun? I'm married! I woke up a little freaked I asked the Lord why am I dressed like this, what does this all mean? He answered daughter remember your vocation. I want you to remember what I taught you. then He said again, remember your vocation.

This vision last Christmas at the midnight Christmas Mass, my husband and I got there early like we always do, the church was so dark and very empty, all of the priests are still asleep before the mass, and I was praying the rosary. When I was finished my husband came back he started praying the rosary. I was praying some more with my husband, and then I heard voices in the vestibule a man and woman. I looked and there was nobody. A few minutes go by then I heard a baby crying in the vestibule, but again there was no one. I thought to myself, what does this mean? Then I heard an ambulance, then I saw the red sirens, it was coming down the church driveway. Then it stopped at the church, I thought it was for real and I thought one of the priest' was having health issues, my husband finished with his rosary.

I asked him to go see where the ambulance is, I told him it stopped in the church parking lot, he went out to the vestibule, and he came back and said there was nobody there was no ambulance out there. I told my priest all about this the next day by e-mail he wrote me back by saying that the baby was the Holy Baby being born the man and woman I heard was the Holy Mother giving birth and Joseph by her side. I think my priest was right but I can't help think about this all of the time.

This vision was before I went to bed: I walked up the stairs I looked out the window on my landing there is a blue light coming from it. Yes! I had to see where it was coming from, this light was so bright, and it lit up my whole driveway. This all happened at night when it is dark, but it was so blue, I looked up in the sky and it was also all blue. I stood there for a while just looking at it. I so badly wanted to go outside, and go into the light, but for some reason I just didn't think I was worthy. And because of that reason, I wasn't sure what would happen to me if I did. It was so crystal water blue and almost as bright as the North Star that I had in another vision. I stopped looking out at the driveway and I went to bed.

This vision was truly amazing: I call it "The Racing Star" I was driving home from my night job, I stopped to get gas for the car, and I looked up in the sky like I always do and I love looking at the stars. Anyhow, I saw this big ball of light just racing across the sky, it circled back around towards me, and then it came down, stayed in the air somehow. And the eyes of the star stared towards me, and it spoke in a male voice. I knew who's star this is I can see His crown of thorns in it. I said Lord why me? Then the star rose back up into the sky, before it was out of sight it said I have to go save my children! Then it picked up speed, it kept rising it went as fast as the speed of light or faster! But it seemed like it was gone in seconds. I told my priest about this one as well but he asked me what do I think it meant? I said that is what my priest is for? He said I have no idea.

This is another vision that was short and at night: I was looking at the stars in the sky; I saw this very bright and very large star off in the distance, like in the north. It was so beautiful I just couldn't take my eyes off it. I went to bed shortly after seeing God's Star, for just a moment I felt like the three kings I even wondered where it shines the brightest and I couldn't help wondering if the Holy Family was at the end of the star again, or still!

There was many different quick moments such as: on Thanksgiving night there was a strong bright light on my stair landing, there is no lamp or wall light there. But it was there for at least a couple of hours in the night time, or this time I was praying to God while I was in bed, I was rising. Where am I going? Then I saw all these hands. Who are they coming from, but they are trying to touch me? I hear singing, voices. I kept rising now I see many faces they are smiling and still trying to reach me, now I see blue sky and many stars, I tried reaching for the sky I looked down at the faces and said am I in Heaven? I started to come down slowly I heard a whisper say yes!

Then I kept coming down and the blue sky was further away. There go the faces then I couldn't hear the voices or the music anymore. I woke up the next morning just wandering, I went to a museum the next day and my priest was there also, we traveled through the museum and I found some paintings of other people's visions and some of them looked just like mine. I told my priest about this and he asked me what does this mean? I just answered, I thought you are the priest and you should tell me, he said something but I can't remember now what it was, I always think about this day.

This vision happened on Halloween night: I originally thought this was a dream, but as it progressed there is no way this is a dream, it started out by me being a specialist. My job is helping the dying clear their minds, souls. and hearts of evil so they will have a safe passing, two of my friends were asking me to help them with a dying friend. This friend refused to let go of his life, he has a disease eating him slowly away through his breathing, his friends say he looks quite grizzly and soon he will not be able to speak or eat! One even said he looks really gross. They even said it is hard to watch or listen to him, they can't stomach it anymore, but this is their friend and they don't want to hurt his feelings so they asked me to help. I did finally agree to help after I asked them, what do you want me to do?

They said, you have got to get him to understand that he doesn't have much time and that he needs to let go and get ready to die! I knew what this meant, but how do you get a person to admit he is dying? It should be obvious right? I asked, why me? There are others like me, the pair said yes! But he asked for you, he asked us to get you I guess he trusts you. So I asked for God's Guidance He told me what to do, then I said take me to him, we got to his house we went in, the place was clean but it smelled like death. It smelled awful, I was afraid to sit anywhere, they didn't tell me what he was dying from.

So I stood the whole time while they called for him. I heard them call out Jim several times, I was fearing that he was already dead; they both went to go find Jim. It turns out that he is having a bad time breathing, he has almost no breathing ability, we must start quickly.

They sat Jim up on a bed up against a wall for support, I looked at him, I said, are you sure you want me? I am not a priest or nun, his friends said he is not of any faith, and he knows you are called by God, he knows you can help, he knows he has no time now, he's as white as a sheet, and his eyes were a sea blue at one time, but they are as white as he is.

So I said a few prayers, called upon God to hear me, and beg forgiveness for Jim because he could not speak any longer. His two friends were sitting on other side of the bed watching. One was holding Jim, and the other is clutching a pillow out of fear, I looked at them both. I said, Jim needs you two also to say these prayers for him. We chanted in Latin it is an old Jewish prayer for the dying. When we finished, I asked Jim, are you ready to go see Jesus, are you ready to go home to God, but most of all are you ready to be judged? Jim was looking up into the sky for a while, then he looked at me and used his eyes to do the speaking as to if say yes!

To all of my questions, Jim said Yes! I said a sendoff prayer in Hebrew, when I was finished, the entire all that was left in this man to help him live, just left him like a slow leaking balloon. When he was gone his eyes were still open. I did close them. I said it is done! His friends said don't worry; he will receive a proper burial. I said this is great! On my way out I closed the door then I went into a shock of my own, I do this every time because I can never believe that I have this ability, I just wonder do I really have this ability, or did God give this to me just for Jim?

This one kind of happened to my husband; he said one night he heard voices coming from me. He told me that I was chanting and I woke him with my chanting, I didn't believe him at first, but he was telling everything I did in the chanting and what he heard. I told my priest about this one as well we asked him what does this mean? He said I have no idea but he said, it's beautiful to think about. I asked my husband, I'm not back to floating in the air, am I? He said no!

This one is very recent: it started with me trying to get to sleep so I was praying to God again. I kept hearing gun shots, but I was too tired to get up and look. I opened my eyes to see if my dog was hearing these shots. no barking. I was about to go back to sleep, then I thought maybe it was my dog and my husband that were shot. But then my dog moved and there was no moaning. I know for a fact that if my dog was shot, he would be yelping loud in pain. But he went back to sleep, and I tried as well. Then I heard a female voice say, no! don't do that! you can't do that! Then I heard more shots, they all sounded very near to my house. But I did find out that there was a murder suicide in my old neighborhood. The husband shot the wife, and then he shot himself. I saw their faces and heard their names and they look and sound familiar to me. But why is this? why I heard the voices and the shots. I have had so many special moments with God. I will treasure every one of them. I pray they keep on coming, everyone one of them is unique and very special to me, because they come from the Almighty One. God.

MY X-MAS TREE CAT

BY BERNADINE ZIEGLER
(12/19/14)

My cat and his brother were very young when we brought them home, we didn't have much, but around Christmas time we put up a used tree. One morning, my husband and I got up and we could not find our boys. I finally looked in the tree then I saw two pairs of sweet little eyes looking out at us saying here I am! From then on we left the Christmas tree up so they both can be with the Baby Christ.

This was so beautiful to me, the boys are older now, but every year, every day of the year, my cat named Radar always visits his Christmas tree no matter what time of the year it is: no matter day or night but he always looks at it like he sees the Christmas Light. Every time he visits his tree I can't help but think about his first memory, and then I smile. I just feel so warm inside I beam with pride and say this is my cat.

My family as in my animals has increased to say the least five cats including my Radar, and a dog named Oscar. They all like to visit and look up at the tree but Radar doesn't let them look for too long, he chases them all away to say this is my tree, this is my Christmas tree. This is so very beautiful to me; I often think how can this be? I have never had a Christmas tree cat.

There have been times I wanted to take his tree down to clean and put it away, but my little white Radar cat will stalk, and stare at you as to ask what are you doing? You will not take down my Christmas tree! I still sneak in the room to clean it but he still watches over the Birth of the Baby Christ and waits to see His Holy Christmas Light, when I see this I think shouldn't we all take a message from my cat, should we be all like this throughout the whole year?

NATURE HIS CREATION

BY BERNADINE ZIEGLER

(2/28/15)

His Nature His Creation, I imagine you all think you know which way this poem is going to go, but do you really know or you just want to be in the show? His Nature His Creation is everything you see from all the waves of grain to the shining seas, from the apples and peaches from His many trees so green, so tall I just love them all, even the many colors of the leaves. The flowers for the bees to pollinate, so you see we must stop all evil before it is too late.

The fun shapes of clouds in the sky as they release rain or snow: they are really His Frozen Tears. Why do we insist on making Him cry? How can you be so cold? Oh me, oh my! How worthy am I to be able to look upon this Great Earth that God has graced and Entrusted to us. Tell me Lord, what is my true worth? Once I saw His Blue Light, Heaven's Blue Light, it was so bright to my surprise it was in my drive-way. I so wanted to step in to the Blue Light but all I could do was stare and pray, why me Lord, why am I worthy?

The sun to keep us warm, the moon to light the night, oh, how you shine so bright! The stars; how they hang in the air, how do they hang on so tight? Oh, how I have got to stop and stare! Somehow when I look up, I just don't have a care, once I saw a racing star! This racing star stopped and turned and then stared at me. I heard it speak to me while suspended in air. The feeling I had you can't compare. I know what or who this racing star is. It is He, The Great I Am, oh! Can you imagine the peace that came over me? The rocks, the stories they could tell if you would only open your heart to hear their voice and the many caves to shelter us from man's cruel harm.

I ask all of you, why must we let evil destroy His Nature His Creation, don't you understand? We are all victims of our own choices. He knows we are not perfect but we all are made in His Likeness, so every choice you make has its own consequence. So I ask all of you raise up your voices, change your choices before His Nature, His Creation is all gone. Bye, bye.

ONE VOICE

BY BERNADINE ZIEGLER
(2-21-13)

My husband sometimes thinks I'm crazy, I asked him why do you say that? He said, if you are not, then why do you write about some very odd things? I asked such as? Creatures and critters: I said poems can be about anything.

Oh! Let me see you wrote a poem about a shoe, a phone, I said those were for fun. What about trees and so many other things? I responded by saying each one of my poems helps me see the sun.

My husband asked me, why do you write about so many living breathing things? I simply said everything that breathes, everything that moves, every living thing feels pain, in this we are the same, I just want them to have a voice that we can all hear, every living thing is a part of God and He is the One Voice we all need to hear.

PARENTS

BY BERNADINE ZIEGLER
(1-28-11)

My parents as a child? No! That is really hard to understand and impossible to imagine, they had to make some hard choices on their own just to become your parents that you will never comprehend, and somehow they always have a guiding loving hand.

Some choices they made are a bit tough, and on you may be a bit rough. Why me, why are you tough on me, you ask? Then when you are almost grown, you want to say, I give up, I had enough but you don't, you ask yourself, why don't I?

As an adult, you finally discover the choices that they had to make, the ones that took you to your brink, you finally comprehend by saying the choices they made really were not so bad, they worked with everything they had, because they love you so. No, that shouldn't make you sad, it really isn't so bad, and it makes you strong to live a whole life long.

The parents never seem to have much, and life is always rough, but they gave you everything they had, and now today when you travel to see your parents you say to yourself, I finally understand, and you become joyous you become voiceless, then you shout out to your mom and dad, "I love you" and "thank you for everything you do" not just for me but for everybody.

Parents, you have got to love them not just because God gave them to you because they molded you into what you are today. And now as a parent yourself you think while laughing, and they say while sitting and watching, now let's see what you can do, after everything you have put us through!

POLLUTION

BY BERNADINE ZIEGLER
(10/30/13)

What is pollution really, what causes it? When I hear this word it just doesn't sound clean, sometimes I just can't figure out how or why does pollution get started? Why do people pollute, as far as I can tell, it is caused by people who are down on their luck. They have to eat on the run because they live on the streets. So they just toss their trash anywhere, they want never to have a home, never to have a buck to their name and being poor will always be their shame. So when they toss the trash forever to remain, and people just stop and stare or just walk on by, they may even do the same thing.

Pollution can be caused in so many ways, not just by people's trash alone. It is also caused by factories poisoning the air and seas, all you can really do is drive by and watch stuff come out of the building's flue but what can we really do to stop this destruction. Why don't people understand, why won't man just take a stand and finally say that is enough, stop your poison flow and clean this place up! Keep in mind God Entrusted us with His World not to have a good time, so I say again; clean it up!

When I was in school, I drew a picture on pollution. I even received an A on it. I wish I got to keep it so I could have started a campaign to clean up God's Creation, but sadly there would always be another person or way to cause more pain, sorrow, and destruction to his beautiful Creation he made for us not to abuse, misuse, or destroy, no! it is for us to live, stop the pollution, for this I plea, you see there is only one solution to the problem and that is to clean up the whole world which is still His and His alone.

PROCRASTINATION

WRITTEN BY BERNADINE MISURA
ON 9-19-06

Procrastination, it knows no destination, it will eat you up starting from outside in, until you figure it out, you don't know how to tell it to go. When you try something new in your life, you try real, hard to strive just to survive, here it comes again to eat you alive, it doesn't care who or where you are, it says you haven't been good at anything so far. you're not going to go very far, so you don't even try, this you cannot deny.

Procrastination is a terrible disease, no, it doesn't make you sneeze or wheeze, it's a lot worse, I know, I am a victim and it has caused a lot of mess and distress in my life, you desperately want to fight it even when you can't see it, you fight it all day and all night, then you figure it out, you have to want to strive in your life to make everything right, no matter your plight.

For this I pray, fight this terrible disease, fight hard, fight strong all day long before it steers you wrong. I beg of you please don't let procrastination eat your soul from within, don't let this awful lying disease win, by never giving in.

SAILING THROUGH HIS TEARS

BY BERNADINE ZIEGLER

(9-20-13)

One day I was looking out on the horizon, I always looked at everything as far as my eyes can see just to thinking about things in my life and what I need to do or what I have left to strive for. Just to chase my cares away, sometimes I would spend the whole day. Then one day I just couldn't stop looking out on the water, and thought where does it come from, where does it all go? How does it flow so slow? What is really all out there?

Then I turned my head just to the left and there was a large white sailing ship, in a ghostly kind of way, why did I not hear it? How did it get here and who did it come for? Who is steering the ship and how? The oddest thing is the sails are in a shape of a cross, there is no engine to make a sound and from what I can see no steering wheel, who is on board, no one that I can see? How could that be?

The horizon is a little foggy in the night. Then I looked to my right side, a man is standing here, who is he? I just couldn't stop looking at him. I finally said to him, did they come for you, who are they, and who are you? I kept thinking as I couldn't stop staring. Then he said quietly, they came for you. I said out of shock for me, why? Why me? He whispered my name and said, child daughter, I am He and I came for you. I asked, why me, Lord?

You would think after I was told that I would go cold with the constant sea breeze, I said the ship! He stopped me and said, it is My Ship, I asked how and who sails it. He smiled, almost laughing at me and said, one of My Chosen! I asked one of Your Apostles, He Turned and

Looked at me while still Smiling. There was a gentle breeze, it touched me just like a warm hand, while I was still at a stand.

I asked, Lord what do You need of me, on the high seas? I asked where did all the water come from, where does it go, He said, someday I will show you the ocean is not water. I looked at Him for a while wondering if the ocean isn't really water then what is it made of? He whispered Tears. I continued to look into His Eyes and He again whispered Tears. I couldn't help but wonder what He meant by that, then just when I was going to ask another question a strong breeze swept across me.

Then He was already gone but the ship, His Ship was already sailing through the Tears, I kept watching the ship travel on the horizon, I shouted out loud whose Tears Lord, is it the sinners tears? I heard him somehow He said, No Daughter! I thought again I heard crying somehow it got louder, it was so loud my ears starting hurting, and then the crying stopped. The ship I can't see any more but somehow I still can Hear Him and I heard Him say, My Tears Child!

I repeated Your Tears. My Lord why, and for who? I cry for all of you because I love you. Why do you not Love Me? Then he said, rather sternly, Why is everyone forgetting About Me? I shouted I have not forgotten my Lord, never will I forget, I do Love Thee, I said out loud then I whispered it again. I just wanted to cry but for some reason I just couldn't, I didn't hear The Voice for a few minutes. He Said the Tears I Shed are because the sinners that do ill will against Me and My Father, The Holy Father of All, He Will Always Extend His Hand for you, this you must and to make others understand.

I Don't Like to Tell any of My Children, away with you, it hurts Me so, I shouted I don't know what to do, I asked, Lord what can I do for you? I don't like hearing you cry, Just the thought makes me die inside,

I just want to make You Happy. He didn't answer me, but I can't help looking out at the horizon. Oh! How I long to be on His Sailing Ship, How I long for Him to come back for Me, I wonder when that will be.

Some time went by He said Help Me by tending all My Sheep and to watch over My Church, telling all My children I have always known of all the wrongs and ill wills committed against My Church and Vessels also help them to understand they can always come back home to Me just by holding out their hand and say Lord please help me! I said Lord, I am unworthy of this honor you ask of me but it will be my joy to help thee.

I asked Lord, how do I do this? He Said, help them travel through the tears by dealing with their tears, then My Tears will be shed no more. This would make my Father and I happy. I said Lord, I am here for you, I will do what you ask of me, to help you by sailing through Your Tears, He whispered to me and said I will be back for you, my daughter. For some reason I just couldn't stop looking out at the horizon.

I just can't help but wonder why people don't understand how they are hurting our Lord by the things they do wrong why can't they realize what pain they are causing our Lord God, why can't they Love Him and His Father, as their Holy Father, as much as I do so you see, He will Always Love all of you and me.

SEEN AND UNSEEN

〰〰

BY BERNADINE ZIEGLER
(11-14-14)

Seen and unseen what does this mean? Why, Oh why! is this so important to me? When the priests say these words, what are they talking
about? Who are they talking about? Will I ever figure it all out? It is
all so confusing to me, how can this be?

For a long time, I could never figure this out. For many years I have tried
I am a Roman Catholic. Oh! How embarrassing for me, so why am I having so much trouble? I feel like I should be hanging from a tree or like I
am stuck in a bubble, oh! What do I do? Please, have mercy on me Lord.

Are the priests talking about The Great Creator, of earth and sky, The
Great Creator of Heaven and hell, The Great Creator of angel and
Man, How can this be? Will I ever understand that God is more than
man. Oh, why do I even try, why must I understand? I think we all
should try to know all we can about the seen and unseen of this world.

Now after all these many years of trying to understand all I can, I finally
get it, you probably are wondering what it is, it is the meaning of everything: His Church, hell, and Heaven, the feeling of peace and happiness that will come over you as it has happened to me. I finally
understand about everything, when the priest says seen and unseen, believe in what they say, all your cares will go away, learn to love the Lord
as I do, because He Loves you too.

I pray someday you all will discover just what this means. I pray you
will find the way His way, the only way and the amazing feelings that
will overcome you, all you have to do is say Lord I believe in you seen

and unseen and always remember He Loves all and He also Loves you. Don't be afraid to say to him, Lord I am sorry for everything I have done and have failed to do, He gives up on no one. God bless you each and every day.

SIX FEATHERS TO THE SON

BY BERNADINE ZIEGLER
(6/6/13)

In the beginning, six feathers were chosen to watch over all His Creation, before they accepted the job; they were told they must stand strong against anyone whom they call an enemy of God. All the chosen feathers swore their allegiance, these six are called to watch over all tribes of all kinds they are His defenders, guardians over all.

The six feathers who stand with the Son, the one that stood up and sensed evil upon us, then it fell apart. The five remaining feathers stood up and said, he is gone. Everyone asked, where did he go? The remaining five said we must do something before we are all gone. What kind of evil force did this, how do we fight it? We must all remain calm and stand strong with The Son.

The fifth feather remained at a stand while looking up and the sky and said, Lord what is this, what is going on? The fifth feather finally said after some time, I am going to do something; I have got to do something! The others said, no! Don't fight it, you will surely die why must you try? The fifth feather said remember your vows; we must fight the evil force but we all must remain strong, he also said, if I don't you will surely be the next, and then the fifth feather was gone.

The fourth feather looked up into the sky and said, my Lord we didn't even get to say good-bye. The fourth one said, I guess I am next to figure out how to fight these evil forces, whatever it may be. It is up to me now, the others said, why no! Not you, you saw what happened to the others do you want this to happen to you too? He said don't you understand we must take a stand and remain strong with The Son. The others said if you leave then there will only be three.

The third feather said to all, that the fourth feather is dead; the remaining feathers said will we never know what is going on. Who is doing all of this? No answer from anyone. The third feather looked up into the sky and said to the Lord, I know it is my turn but why must we all try, we will all die, will we never figure out whom or why this is happening to all of us?

The other feathers asked the third one; what are you going to do, are you going to fight, after some time went by he said, the others went into the day, I am going to find this evil force by night. As he left in the night the last two watched him leave while saying, I guess it's all up to us, but the third one has not died in fact. He did find out about the evil force but he remained hiding in the night light. The third feather figured out what to do but he was unable to return to tell the news, he stumbled and took a great fall, he became broken.

The last two said the third has not returned, I guess it is up to you and I to fix this evil and to struggle through we must survive. The remaining two looked up at the sky and said, we stand with you what must we do? The Lord said, you must destroy all the evil flags they want to take over all of you. They also said we will do whatever it takes no matter what; we must go through no matter if it is a lost cause.

All of the chosen feathers have been destroyed or broken. Who bent them? What can the rest of us do? We said as we looked up into the sky as if to see His Holy Light? He answered we must remain strong and destroy all the different evil flags. The people asked if we don't succeed Lord, what then will happen to the stars up above, the moon and the sun, if they are all gone then so are all of us. The Lord nearly shouted and said no! There is another, and then we all looked down.

There is a light, where is it coming from? I was the first one to look up. There are the six broken feathers standing strong with The Son, at first we couldn't make out what they were saying, then the words became more clear. The Son was saying, all of the feathers are not broken; there is another one among all My Children, you are not done.

We all looked around and said who is the other one? The Son is looking at me, I thought to myself how can this be? I closed my eyes to use my thoughts to speak to The Son, How can this be Lord, how can I remain strong, will I succeed for you? Am I the last one Lord? Can I be the last one to defeat the evil ones? I will do as you say! Lord, I will remain strong I will always stand with you, The Son. Then the sky light went away, I said to everyone, I know what to do! We are victims of our own choices, with every choice there are consequences.

SLOW DOWN THE RAIN

BY BERNADINE MISURA
(10-18-06)

It's so dark out here, what is that I hear, it's five in the morning, God I'm heading off to work could you slow down your rain? All I can see and hear, in front of me in back of me and all round me is the rain, everywhere I go both high and low it is probably even pounding on the window pane.

It is coming down very fast and hard, I finally made it to my car, will it start? As I turned the key, I said car, don't break my heart! And it started, for that I'm glad, and because I don't need to stop for gas. The rain started to slow, I thought not bad. I said while driving away God keep me safe!

Then as I left I muttered here we go, it started again, I said out loud, God, is heaven in this much pain? how do I slow down your rain? It's like a whole bunch of water came from the sky. I dare not ask why, because then he will make it end to never come back again.

It rained all that day and most of the next night, as I went to bed to the sounds of God's rain, I prayed to him. I said, Lord, cleanse my heart and soul with the rain remove all my stain, ease all of my pain and help me sleep peacefully again.

The morning came and to my delight, I sleep soundly all through the night to awake to his beautiful morning light. I looked up into the sky, and I said, Good Morning Lord and to all of you in Heaven, thank you for the glorious sound of the day and the strong warm sun to light my way.

STINEFIELD UNIVERSITY

BY BERNADINE MISURA
(2/25/01)

I received an invitation in the mail to see this new college in my neighborhood, the invitation simply read: Dear Miss Shallow Waters: I, Mr. Stinefield, owner has acknowledged your interest in our school as it was being built. This is why we decided to extend to you this invitation to our open house. It is for one day only and you may bring a guest, I must admit I did watch the building being built that always fascinates me I did wonder what the town of Chastity Ohio, was going to do with this very large piece of property in the middle of the town, so I do want to go I know all colleges are all the same right, but something tells me this one is going to be different. I did however did some exploring before I asked my mother Estelle O'Brite, to come with me since she also at times watched the building being built with me we were both amazed how fast they got it up.

Mother did say she wanted to go to the opening, so I was excited for the day to arrive, it couldn't come fast enough, but it is finally here. When we arrived on foot because the school is very nearby, we were told to find seats in the gym area and that there are also snacks and drinks for everyone who comes, so my mother and I found our seats in the upper bleachers there are a lot of folks here, and from what we can see from our seats the school is very nicely done, the speaker arrived and described the schools lay out and what they are going to teach we both can hear them very well, and to our surprise what type of people will be accepted into this university, I thought just about everyone could be accepted to the colleges but not this one. I thought to myself will mother and I be accepted, after the speakers were done three in all the director came to everyone afterwards and said feel free to have a look around. Stinefield has enough tour guides to show everyone around and to answer any questions you may have.

Mother and I did go on our own after the director left I said we never did get his name but something tells me it was Mr. Stinefield, mom said that is alright we'll get it later, so I just couldn't believe my eyes the whole inside is white but not bright white, the are some pictures on the wall some are of people who help run this school but I did something very odd I was looking down the hallway into the classrooms and I saw a man in mid-air looking out the door but before I saw him and the inside of the classroom.

I saw two very bright lights I think they were pointing the room out to me I thought it was because that is where I might be taking most of my classes after I sign up, the director said they have universities around the world this is the first town in the north east, some other pictures I see in the classroom has a big one of Jesus, nuns, the Holy family separate and together, and some passages from the Holy Bible, the Catholic Holy Bible, I did find this unusual because it's Ohio a state that has thrown out God, and two because Stinefield did not claim to be Catholic based or ran but don't get me wrong I love this idea my family is catholic and we have been and always will be, I have a thought and I voiced it to mother I wonder if any students go on to be priest or nuns, then there was silence again. We continued to walk around it seemed like for hours a tour guide came our way and before we could see her face she asked us is there anything we have to ask or want to see? She finally got close enough to hear our answers to her question mother and I said yes! We would like to see more as she kept talking to mother I kept thinking to myself I know this woman it did take me a while but I figured it out it is my old childhood friend Katherine Hazzard, I haven't seen her in many years, since high school. I thought to myself I always wondered what happened to her.

Katherine asked mother if she was interested in the programs for the elder students she also said since you are the first one on opening day we will set you up even if you are the only one for the classes for the elders, okay she said Estelle, mother seemed happy with that offer

Katherine said to me I'll be back this will take a few minutes she said look around some more I acknowledged what she said but after Katherine set up mother with her program in computers, for the elders, mother must of went home because she didn't come back with Katherine, when Katherine came back to me she asked me what I would be interested in studying I didn't get to answer I said out loud Katherine Field, is that you where have you been?

Katherine muttered Oh! Long story lets show you around through the rest of the school, like the dorm rooms and some of the students who have already arrived. I looked at my invitation again and thought to myself is she Stinefield's daughter and he just combined his two names together, I said Katherine why is there so many dorms in this very large school she smiled and said that is why because it is easier for the students to go to their dorm right after their classes most of them are very tired and they need to study a lot and also always need a tutor around which one is provided for morning through the night. We saw many dorms most were empty then we came to one about in the middle of this long hallway Katherine said you may remember this man it was Brian Unger my old boyfriend it didn't end well.

It finally dawned on me what they are studying here Brian has special gifts from The Holy Spirit, I thought this out to myself, I finally said out loud Katherine what is being taught here? Yes! I know Brian and I also know that he was given a special gift from God; He can levitate, and make things come to him just by looking at it. Before she answered me she took me to another dorm it was empty except for some things like books clothes like a uniform and a map of the school but they also had my name on them but I haven't signed up yet, I said kind of shockingly Katherine what is this stuff and why does it have my name on it?

She said this is God's university this school is for God's chosen people who receive graces from Him we teach everyone here how to use them and when not to use them also many other subjects such as business, and law, among many and we teach you how to use them in your chosen careers, I thought about what she said then I said so does this mean you have a special grace she said yes! I can heal with a touch of my hands; I thought to myself then said out loud I heard you are married. She got quiet on me she whispered in a sober voice Yes! He is dead I couldn't save Jim Hazzard right she whispered Yes! Again while turned away Katherine went on to say I got there too late to do anything I said I'm sorry Katherine I had no idea. I also asked what does this all have to with me she smiled at me with tears in her eyes and said Shallow don't you know that you have at least three maybe more of His graces, you should have been here before me.

I asked harshly Katherine where is my mother and for what did she enroll? Katherine was surprised by my tone she said don't worry in a happier tone, she will be along soon she signed up for the computer classes we offer for the students in her age bracket which is sixty plus. Then all of a sudden here comes mother, Katherine looked and said there she is Miss Estelle, she seems real happy so I calmed down mother even said to me calm down Shallow this school is cool you will fit right in and shouted mother I haven't signed up yet! I must admit to myself at least I feel pretty excited about all of this but I still don't want to show that feeling yet. Miss Estelle hugged Katherine like she knew her I said mother do you know this lady she said yes! This is your friend from grade school I was shocked I said mother how do you know this I never told you about her, she answered and said that is my special grace, mothers' intuition. How many times have I heard that before I thought to myself?

We all arrived at Katherine's dorm room it is one of the first set of dorms, she said can we stop for a while my feet are on fire we all said yes! At the same time I said I'm a little hungry also, all the dorms look the same all white fully decorated, the students names are on the doors, I finally agreed to sign up for law, business and theology on the side. We stayed there for a couple of hours then Katherine said there are only a few more dorms to see. I said to her can we skip seeing those dorms? But I also want my dorm to be towards the end, I am not a fan of noise. I want quiet so I can pray to God in peace. Katherine said sure with some digress, but I didn't care, she also said that Brian is down there, I said oh!

Yeah you are going to move him towards your dorm he just would be in my way. She took some time then she finally said of course we can do that he didn't like being down there by himself anyway. I said great then it is settled. I asked one final question I said where is the church in here or do you have one? Katherine said no we don't have one yet but there are a couple of churches nearby that we attend, that is also why we give every student an hour and a half for all the masses, and walking back to the school, she went on to say as for Bible study we do a lot in the classes because everything we teach here is for God. I said that sounds good Katherine I also said it really has been good to see you also, that seemed to of cheered her up just a little.

Two hours went by Katherine put her shoes back on and said we had better finish up I got up first I was a little anxious oh! Who am I kidding I am a lot of bit anxious, Katherine got up and said shallow I have to talk to you about something I said alright what is it? She said we have to go back to the dorm we chose for you first and we will talk on the way there she said that there is a problem a small one, I thought to myself here it comes I hear this line a lot also, Katherine said there can be no hatred in here not for any person or from any person your relationship with Brian didn't end well right? I said right! She said well we have to have both of you go through a sort of court case with a jury of the universities peers, I was trying to figure out in my head what she is talking about then I finally said out loud Huh! Katherine what are you talking about? The court cases are like a cleansing of old bad emotional baggage.

We arrived at that pre-assigned dorm everything is the same as before but this time I see my bible from my bedroom in my current house with my mother I picked it up to make sure I looked through it and I was right it is my Bible then I saw another book a smaller one I knew what book this is also I said very angrily it is my diary, I looked at their faces and they both have the look of fear I said what is this doing here and said quite strongly, mother did finally answer after a slight pause she said Katherine called me and asked me to send your diary over before we arrived here for the opening you can't imagine how angry I got I shouted you did what?

You went into my personnel space the house I bought so you can live with me you went into my bedroom and went through my things how dare you! Katherine said Shallow don't be angry with Miss Estelle, mother chimed in and said when Katherine explained the reason to me it sounded real good Katherine continued to say if you must be angry with someone let it be with me not you mother, I must admit I did try to calm down because I love my mother dearly. I asked did anyone else see this? Then I hear a male voice laughing oddly, I looked through it to see if anything is missing and nothing seems to be missing I looked at those two and said I am still very angry at you nut let's move on.

Then it happened I was about to leave with the rest of the tour I turned around there was Brian looking at me face to face laughing and smiling just like a man up to a devilish trick, I said kind of softly what do you want you four eyed pond scum, he didn't say a word but he wouldn't move out of my way either I thought to myself you have the nerve to still exist, but I did push my way through somehow. I put my head up high then I realized somehow I am standing in a courtroom a case is going on who's is it better yet how did I get here where is the tour I was about to leave with?

I heard his voice I turned around it is Brian, I stood there like a stone afraid to move it seemed like a long time but for a couple of minutes, I sat down at a large square table a lawyer is sitting there motion me over by calling my name I said who is this man this attorney I finally decided to listen to the case Brian was called to the stand and I heard him say I did nothing that has been claimed by Miss Waters or what has been written by Miss Waters, I was about to shout out some unkind words but the attorney stopped me and whispered relax! You got him dead to right, so I sat back down watching Brian in the witness stand I said to myself is this some kind of a bad dream?

Then it became my turn to be called to the stand I did everything such as the swearing in and then sitting down in the witness chair I was asked many questions about the relationship by I guess my attorney first then Brian', the last thing I remember saying is that I just want to go on with my life and to let Brian Unger go on with his life because I don't need him and he didn't do anything wrong mentally or physical just judgment wise like all men do, they run off with someone that they think is better than the lady they are with they find out otherwise that their choice was wrong.

I didn't get to hear the judgment against Brian but I also didn't really care either, then somehow I was back in the gym sitting on the bleachers with mother like nothing ever happened, I don't understand why isn't anybody else reacting like I am I said come on mom lets leave the tour I have had enough of this mother was trying to say something while I rushed her out of there before she could say something I said mother they are acting like we have been there in those bleachers the whole time. We got outside mother looked at me oddly because of what I said she asked shallow are you feeling alright.

I thought to myself did I just go through a port hole I feel like I went through a time warp of some kind I think it is kind of strange that mom isn't feeling like I am, I finally turned around to get one last look at Stinefield University I can't believe my eyes there is nothing there but one big empty piece of property where did the school go where could such a large building go and where are all the folks I thought to myself where did everyone go?

Mom looked briefly and then she said well time to go home! While staring at nothing I whispered yeah! I guess so I'll be right there, but I just couldn't help but wonder, was this even real did any of it really happen was I even in a school or courtroom, I return to my house and bedroom and everything that was at the school is here back in my room, I just don't understand I thought to myself I looked at the Crucifix in my room above my headboard. I said are all those people dead? Lord was this a message from you or was it a very odd dream? What does this all mean Lord I don't understand?

THE CLEAR MEDALLION

BY BERNADINE ZIEGLER

(11/17/14)

The clear medallion is my grandfathers. I never met him. If I did I know him, I would never forget him. The clear medallion is etched just like a diamond and the Holy Mother is standing in the middle and a child kneeling at Her Feet, for a long time I couldn't stop looking at it, because of its simple beauty. It seemed like at times all I could see was light, oh! Why does it shine so bright, I could see why grandpa guarded it with his life?

I was told by God that I need to take this medallion to his vessel, the one named Kieran, so he can see and hear the Lords Light with such delight! I know He was right when He Asked me to give Kieran a message and the medallion that glows with His dancing bright light, you should have seen Kieran's eyes, they could have lit up the night with such delight as always. The Lord God is right: Kieran needed to be reminded that the Lord Sees All, Hears All and Knows All and that God Loves him, just like He Loves all of us this you can trust.

I don't regret that I gave away my grandfather's medallion because I know my priest needs it more than I do, I pray he is not so blue any more. God told me the medallion will open up Heavens Door for him so he can hear and see so much more than what he reads and prays to us about, I pray the medallion will help Father Kieran figure it all out.

You would think a priest would already have all the answers, and for this reason, they cry in silence even though they know all the Lords Laws and written words. Remember they are still human and need our help to understand all about the one known as I Am. Could you at least try and stand by your priests side, so they don't have to feel like they are so alone and trapped from inside. The very thought of this hurts me to the bone.

THE DARK WALL

BY BERNADINE MISURA
(7-21-06)

The dark wall, I can never take my eyes off, why I ask? It goes on and on that is all I can see on one side, the other walls are as white as snow they even seemed to flow in the sky but I do not know how or Why?

I see on the dark wall a bunch of little lights they burn so bright just like the stars in the sky at night, I heard a voice say those are not little lights! I thought to myself they may not be, but they are still a delight for me to see.

There is one that shines so bright I can't see
I think how that can be it seems like it is coming from the north, but pointing to the east. Where am I? Why me?

I think to myself again am I in the sky how I can't fly?
How I'm just a human kid I think again am I
Dead? If I am then why can't I move where I stand?
Something is holding me I can't feel "ah" my hand,

I am with two other people a man, and a lady, they answered me by saying. "It's not your time". I asked what do you mean? I don't understand; they both said don't worry you need not be in a hurry. I think for what if I'm not dead.

While I am waiting for what? Whom? I do not know every time I come here I can't help but look around I do my best not to make a sound, then I look at the guy, and the lady, I finally said every time I come here so do the both of you, why?

I asked who are the both of you? They both said you are just like us but our times are almost up. I did ask how many times have you been up here we all said three. I still had to think about where we are. I asked after some time had gone by are we in heaven? No answer.

Again I looked around still not making a sound, but I did hear other voices laughing, giggling, having fun, they're getting louder, and stronger, I kept looking I couldn't help it there are some beams of lights floating around they are so bright some are even behind me and touching me how can that be? I wanted to scream, but a man in all white came in, I tried to laugh quietly, his beard was even all white and it dragged across the floor as he walked with his white cane,

The man spoke and I thought out loud the voice is His Voice; he answered all my thoughts and questions by saying yes! You are all in heaven! Before I could ask why he said wait rather sternly, with his cane he said the lights touching you are his angels, I am his voice. He told me his name, but he also said not to tell anyone who will not arrive here. He also said man will continue to play his evil game, and mankind, must destroy his Holy Name.

Then he looked at me, I said I'm frightened, he replied don't be. There are so many, he said just stay with me and the one we know and love as He. The man said you are waiting on your body to finish its fight. He finally said after some time it's ready you may now take your flight back down.

I have been down here for many years now and I have not told anyone about my flights, or those heavenly lights, but I will always remember my holy friends I pray someday but not today, I can dance and sing with them when it will be my end, that would be a joyous day I pray will never end.

THE DEAD SEA SCROLLS

BY BERNADINE ZIEGLER
(3/16/15)

The Dead Sea Scrolls: What are they? What do they contain, what are they really made of? Does anyone really know? Has anyone really seen them, can anyone tell me if they really exist? Who wrote them and why did they hide them and from whom? What kind of life did they lead? To where they would have to hide these ancient and possible Holy Words wrapped in earthen ware in a cave from nowhere. Why doesn't anyone care?

What is the real importance of these words? Why have the words that contain them not been revealed to the world, don't you want to know? I do, Oh! How I would like to see them to feel them to know why these scrolls needed to be in hiding is it because the writer was dying and there was no one to carry on the writing. Why isn't anyone wondering? Why isn't anyone wondering if the scrolls contain the Blessed Words of God, I so want to know?

Does't anyone of you wonder what was so important to write down, but not important enough for anyone else to know? I heard that they have been found, so I ask where are they now? Can anyone figure out what they say: Are they messages from the Lord? Since they have been found, where did they go? Will we ever know, will we ever know what this all means, why do they call them the Dead Sea Scrolls anyway? I was just wondering.

THE DEFENDER
OF HISTORICAL TRUTH

BY BERNADINE MIISURA
(8-26-06)

What is historical truth you ask? Well, I don't claim to know everything, because one can't know everything except the Good Lord, I do know history is part of the past, even our past, yes! A lot of it will always remain a mystery.

Yes! Some of the history as we know has been really bad, but without it, what and where would we be? Then what have you really learned? If you think you can do better than the people of the past, that would be news to me, there is a lot of good history that is quite a puzzle. But for me, I will defend all historical truth, and I don't need proof: I have God, The Lord Jesus, His Son, The Holy One, The Great I Am.

He tells me what is true or not, being loved by Him, believe me that is more than enough to know what is right and wrong in our lives. Now and in the unchangeable past, history cannot be changed so stop your complaining about what is wrong with the world. Stop trying to change God's World and fix all of your wrongs and make them right.

Tell everyone God's Son is coming, and if you keep on with your evil ways you will also be part of the past, the bad history. Get down on your knees and pray to God and say Lord God I Love and Adore thee, please save me, I don't want to become history without the Love of Your Son the Holy Christ, please forgive me!

You do this and just like me you will become a defender of the historical truth, the historical truth is and always will be Named God the All Mighty maker of Heaven and Earth, Seen and Unseen, and Don't you forget it!

THE FALL

BY BERNADINE ZIEGLER
(1-28-13)

As I am standing watching the leaves come down, it doesn't make me happy, why, you ask? I answered it means my friends are going away to come back some other day, you ask who are my friends, and why are they going away? I simply say the sun, the moon, the rain and the stars.

The falling of the leaves means they have to leave no rain to wash away my pain, and strain of the day, as for the moon and stars, I won't be able to see. Please God don't let me fall to the dark abyss You and Your Beautiful Living Gifts I will forever miss.

My days will be the longest nights, there will be severe cold, severe wind, oh, my howling from within, and the snow is on the way, the snow used to be my friend and someday maybe again when I can finally play all day, as for now they just bring me strain and pain, God, if you feel you must, I say Okay.

I know and love Ohio but, when I have to drive to a special occasion, I want the snow, cold, and wind to go away because of all the natures winter frustrations, oh, who am I kidding? I love Ohio, and even all the colors of God's Nature Show.

As long as I have God on my side, I even will say good-night and good-bye to my loyal friends, I will see you again, I will love it even when the leaves fall, I'll make do with all the wonders of the outside.

When I see the snow, I'll make a wish that I could be a child again, just for one day forever to race and play in the snow, as I'm sliding down the hills I shout woo woo! I love you Lord God! And all of the many colors of Ohio's beautiful and never ending terrain.

THE FORGOTTEN SOULS
(As told through the eyes of a slave)

∼∼

BY BERNADINE ZIEGLER
(1/11/12)

This is a story about a young boy, in Fortune Mississippi, not just any boy; he is now six years old. He is also a black boy right after slavery ended, but Mississippi never did sign into law. The year is 1869, slavery ended in 1865. He and his mother Monica Moses were set free. His father Maurice Moses, was always a free man: at least since his son was born. Leonard was born Leonard Charles Moses, in 1863 just two years before slavery ended, times were really hard for his mother but they stayed with their original owner until the government told him they must leave because they are free now, Monica had no idea why they should leave.

If they wanted to stay there and they were also wanted by the ranch owner: he was also black but he was a foreigner to the states. He had no idea how to run a ranch by himself. But they were told to leave or he will be charged or put in prison. Monica didn't want that for Joseph, she had no choice then to move on, so things got really tough not just for the Moses family but for all the freed slaves, they had nowhere to go, so they had to find where they could go: a place on the street or broke down unattended houses or ranches, no money no food since they were slaves, no education except for a select few.

As Monica and her son Leonard fled from the ranch that they once called home, Maurice ran from there years back because he was receiving most of the whippings from Joseph more than Monica or even their child. Joseph didn't believe in hitting children no matter what race they come from, when Monica left the ranch all she could see are people of all kinds running about, she stopped for a bit she saw the beautiful light shining in front of her. While she was still and looking at the beautiful lady in the light Leonard asked momma where are all these people going to go, what is going to happen to us? Monica didn't answer at first Leonard tapped her arm a few times, Monica had no answers she closed her eyes briefly; she opened them to say I don't know! I just don't know! The light was dissipating Monica had no idea why only she saw the Lady of the Light.

They continued to walk but to where? Out of the blue Maurice appears, this shocked Monica, and she asked angrily where have you been? Where have you been for years? Maurice saw his child; it seemed like to him for the first time. He asked is this Leonard my boy? Maurice kept looking at him he has always been unsure of this because Leonard has blue eyes: bluer than all the seas, and on a black boy child, never ever has been heard of or seen. Monica almost smiled but said, yes Maurice! This is your son! Maurice said I have a place. I found a place but we must leave town now! He went to say that it is an abandoned ranch, lots of land, only one neighbor they are also slaves' no-free slave from a different race, this confused Monica, but she just wanted to get to shelter, so she let him lead the way.

It seemed like they were walking for hours and all Monica saw on the way was land almost no people she asked Maurice are we almost there? My feet are hurting and Leonard is tired, Maurice said yes Mamie we are here she looked up to see a lot of land it went on for miles as far as the eye could see there is a wood fence broke in some places everything grown over there is a lot of work to be done the house looks old and ran down Monica hopes that it is good enough to live in she even asked Maurice if the house is strong enough he said oh yes! Mamie it looks weak but sturdy, she asked where are we?

Maurice said Mercyville Mississippi, abouts 30 miles south of Fortune City where they came from. Maurice took them inside to look around and to show them a place where they can lay down and nap for a spell, and they both fell asleep on the floor where they usually do sleep, Maurice covered them and then closed the door quietly, when they awoke they looked around the old ranch to see what will needs to be done or what and where to grow food and maybe have some farm animals someday, Monica said this will take a lot of work to fix this place up, can we do this? Maurice said it will be lots of work. Yes Mamie it will work.

Monica brought up the fact that she would like to get Leonard and herself some book learning some how can I get some book learning where do I go she said to Maurice he said not sure but he did see a burnt out church it was the First Methodist church it was turned into a school I saw kids go in there, it was abouts 5 miles out from here due north, I think it is called now St. Martin, Monica asked do you think they will take Leonard and teach him? He said I dun know Mamie but you can have a look see in the morning, she thought to herself out loud I wonder if there is a church around these parts.

Maurice heard her and couldn't believe his ears he shook his head and went to see where he can start on the land, before he got out of ear shot, she shouted out have you seen any church around here? He didn't answer not just because he didn't look because he has never been to a house of worship or anywhere where there is book learning, reading of any kind Monica understands his frustrations, but she was around their ranch owner a lot and he taught her some reading, writing, spoke to her about God and Jesus His Son, and a lady named Mary, and a virgin who had a baby this also confused Monica I guess she just wants to figure out how a woman can have a baby without a man, she knows there has got to be more to the story. Monica dare not tell Maurice about the Lady of the Light, he would not understand what she saw but she thinks that a preacher man would know the answers she is seeking.

Monica set out the next day to check out the school Maurice spoke about she walked on foot so she could get there faster and she wasn't sure of the schools location it didn't take Monica to long to walk that far but it did take her a while to find the school, nobody but the teacher was there so she walked up to the school a bit leery after all it was just yesterday the slaves were let go. Monica was sure news didn't travel that fast, the teacher addressed her in a proper fashion just like anyone else. The teacher was dressed in all white from head to toe her hair was covered up, all that was visible is her eyes and they are brown, when she introduced herself.

She said hi with a smile and her hand out she said my name is Ms. Jones; Monica seemed at ease so she asked Ms. Jones, if her son a free slave boy can get some book learning here at St. Martin, Ms. Jones still smiling said Yes Ma'am! Ms. Jones went on to say all children of any race are welcome here at St. Martins, this made Monica relieved Monica also said I have no money to pay! Ms. Jones said all children are welcome here even the poor, Ms. Jones did say when you do acquire some money St. Martins only asks you to donate to the school when you can. No matter how much just donate what you can afford alright, this made Monica beyond happy for her son but what about her Monica did ask Ms. Jones if she can acquire some book learning also Ms. Jones said I'll have to tutor you after the day classes are over Monica said you would do that for me? Ms. Jones said Yes Ma'am, I would!

And she said bring your son early tomorrow and we'll get things started. With Ms. Jones gentle shake of Monica's hand to bid her good bye Monica curtsied to her and said, Ms. Jones one more question if you please is there a church I may go to around here? Ms. Jones said yes! St. Martin also has a church about a mile down the road behind the school, Monica curtsied to Ms. Jones again and said thank you Ma'am, see you in the morning.

Monica was so happy walking home she thought to herself things may not be good all the time but they are right now, she was looking forward to telling Maurice the news but she couldn't help wondering will he be pleased, unhappy or a shamed because he still doesn't have any book learning, but she just wanted to be happy now for at least a little while. When she got home Maurice was tending the land prepping it for what they might be growing, Monica went into the house to check on Leonard, he is fine that also made Monica pleased so she went out to the porch with a drink and sat on a very old chair. It needed some tending just like the rest of the property. So this made Monica wonder again if Maurice was going to be angry with her because she will be getting some book learning also and maybe not doing a lot of chores when Maurice may want them done.

Maurice saw that Monica was home so he stopped his work temporarily but he wanted to hear her news before sun went down, he came to her sat down and said so what's the news? She said I found the school and the teacher said I can send Leonard to school she also said no moneys required then she paused and said the teacher Ms. Jones also said I could be tutored if I would like when Monica said this she feared his anger, but there wasn't any he was just silent but she didn't dare tell him that she found a church, Monica asked him so what you think? Maurice answered after a spell he finally said when can he start school?

She said in the morning, Tomorrow. He asked how are you going to tell Leonard? She looked at him and said with a smile you're not mad? He said with a slight smile no Mamie! I'm fine she asked softly and about me being tutored? He asked where, at the school or here? Monica said not sure didn't ask, he said softly if here think she will teach me also? Monica had the biggest smile and said I'll ask Ms. Jones in the morning, Maurice said I best get back to work before night fall he got up Monica still was smiling while watching him part from the house and thought to herself I don't dare tell him I found a church to attend she thought to herself I'll let him find the church for himself so he doesn't feel like he is being forced to do anything. Monica didn't want that for him. She just got her husband back after all these years: she didn't want to lose him now; she and Leonard need him now more than ever.

Morning came early for Monica, so how she had to convince Leonard to get up to go somewhere that he has never been, it turns out it wasn't as hard as she thought for a six year old boy. Leonard was getting bored just being around the old abandoned ranch. Monica was taking

Leonard to the school St. Martin's, when Monica got to the doorway, she looked in and this time there are a group of children, some white, some darker in skin tone but not as dark as Leonard, some were even red skinned, the teacher Ms. Jones saw Monica and Leonard at the doorway she said while motioning to them come on in all are welcomed here she smiled at Leonard and said come Leonard join us take a seat don't be afraid! Monica whispered to her son and said it'll be okay son Ms. Jones is nice, with some fear Leonard took a seat in the front row because there was only one left of ten seats, Ms. Jones whispered to Monica don't worry he will be fine.

Monica was about to leave and Ms. Jones said to her I'll walk him home and come tutor you, Monica motioned with a bow and said Ms. Jones may I ask a question? Ms. Jones came towards Monica so she can whisper her question she asked if she would tutor her husband also because he would like to book learn also but he has fear to ask, Ms. Jones smiled and said that will be fine, Monica set on for home to help Maurice with the chores before they both hear about Leonard's first day at school, Monica didn't know if she should feel happy or have fear so she muttered to herself I guess alls I can do is pray. She prayed all the way home the whole five miles, time went by so fast by the time she looked up she was already home.

When she got home Maurice was already working the land he stopped working so he can hear about the school journey Leonard took and to see if Ms. Jones will give him book learning also, Maurice was so excited because he found some alfalfa still growing even though the land went unattended for a spell, he told Monica about this he also said that it is healthy and there will be enough to harvest for some money, this made the both of them so happy. Monica also told him her good news that Ms. Jones agreed to teach him also.

Maurice was happy but surprised. She also said that she will teach here so we can learn in silence, while they were embracing each other some people approached them, three people of a different color and race: a couple and a boy, to Monica they were even dressed oddly, with feathers in their hair they said howdy told the Moses, Monica and Maurice said that they are the neighbors and to ask them if they could keep their where abouts quiet and their names because they are still slaves, they have not been freed, Monica and Maurice were shocked at this news.

I think Monica didn't believe them but agreed anyway, the parents also asked if they knew where there is a school that will teach their son the white man's ways. They went on to say if their son is in school and they are caught and taken back to their owner if the Moses would watch over their son for a spell and take care of him? Monica said yes! To the neighbors but still with some duress, but she was raised to always be willing to lend a hand to anyone who asked for help, her mother said that is the Christian way.

Meanwhile, this was going on at the house, Monica couldn't help worrying about Leonard and how he is doing, Ms. Jones asked all the children to say their names out loud to everyone and tell something about themselves to the other children when it became Leonard's turn he introduced himself just fine but then he paused because he was trying to think of something else to say then just out of the blue he started reciting an old poem his grandmother taught him to ease the tension in the room when there is nothing to say, it is called the Nanny Goat, it goes like this: once upon a time, the goose drank wine, the monkey chewed tobacco on the street car line, the street car broke, the monkey choked and they all went to heaven on a nanny goat! Leonard doesn't know what any of it means but somehow he always gets a laugh when he recites it and he did this time all well, Ms. Jones said very good Leonard while still laughing and said take your seat so he did, but for some reason Leonard couldn't help having the feeling that not everyone likes him, but in his silence he did thank his grand mama's memory.

Time seemed to have gone by so fast Ms. Jones rang the bell, and said class dismissed. All the kids were leaving to go to their homes. Leonard was also about to leave, Ms. Jones said wait Leonard I'll walk you home! She got her things and her books for tutoring but she dare not tell Leonard the real reason why she is walking him home, she took his hand started walking towards his house, she asked Leonard so how did you like your first day of school? Leonard didn't answer her for a spell in his silence he was wondering why Ms. Jones was walking him he was thinking is it because I'm dark, Leonard finally did ask this very question with shock Ms. Jones stopped, bent down to his level and said don't ever think that way Leonard we all are not like that and everyone in your class is not like that she gently rubbed his face and said do you understand Leonard? Everyone in the class has the same situation as you; the only difference is the color of your skin. But the color of your skin will never matter to me; she asked him again do you understand? He gave a somber yes head gesture. Ms. Jones continued to say Leonard I know you are new to this but I want you to know that I love all my kids, I love all my students, she dried his tears she said don't worry you never have to worry she said again don't worry. Okay?

They continued to walk to Leonard's house Leonard did finally asked teacher, why are you really walking me home? At this moment she knew she had to think fast she finally asked him do you really know your way home? After all you do live much further away than the other children; you are new to the neighborhood. Ms. Jones turned and smiled at Leonard and said how about we say that I worry about all my children then she bent down and whispered your mother asked me to make sure you make it home and if you like I would like to walk you home every day but only if you would like.

He seemed a lot more relaxed and happy also, he whispered I did like being with all the different kids he asked can I come back tomorrow? She bent down to his size and said you can come to the school every day if you like and you wish to talk to me after school time come to the school anyway I'll be here Okay. He looked up at her as to say yes! To both of their surprise they have arrived at his house, she said where did the time go? Ms. Jones looked around with her eyes and whispered your parents do have a lot of work to do, she looked him in the eyes and said lets get you in your house they were walking closer to the house Miss Monica waved her hand while trying to call out her name for her to hear, but Monica was really telling Maurice this is the teacher honey stop working your son is home.

Maurice stopped his work he seemed to be more excited to see his son than Monica but they're both very happy to see him and would love to hear about his first day, Maurice never told Monica but he has been looking forward to this ever since she told him about the school allowing his son, in his silence he is even more excited to be book learning, he has always wanted to learn and maybe he is a little jealous of his own son. Maurice was the first one there to greet him and hug his son for the first time in Leonard's life, they asked Ms. Jones to stay for supper but they didn't say anything in front of Leonard about why she is really here. She stayed and after Leonard went down for a nap, Ms. Jones took her opportunity to start teaching the both of them first thing she did was to give them a test to check what level of learning they are at, but Maurice has never been exposed to a book but Monica on the test was at a much higher level, Then she started Monica on her own and worked with teaching Maurice how to read first thing.

There was a couple of times he got a little upset but Ms. Jones knew how to get him back to trying and he nearly read a whole book out loud. Both of the ladies where very proud of him and they showed it, this made him so at ease. Monica noticed Maurice's beautiful smile she never saw it before it took her by surprise, so surprised they didn't see their native neighbors slowly walking up and watching them at the same time when they finally got into the eyes sight of the Moses family the teacher was gone they startled Monica, their neighbors still didn't give them any name to call them because they are still in hiding so Monica just said yes! To them the father of the family had his hands on their son and said we saw you had a teacher over here. Is there any way we could get her to teach our boy? We are not inquiring for us, but we do want a better life for our boy may we please ask for your help to get our boy the proper learning?

They all said please at this time, Monica said yes but he will have to learn at the school St. Martins, it is five miles out. Maurice said you will have to help with the ranch because you are living in the little house that comes with ours, the parents said anything you all have been so kind to us and we are forever grateful. Monica said to the mother that she would talk to the teacher if the lady of the house would go with her. The mother seemed stand offish at this the native couple had a talk in their language, she finally said to Monica, afterwards that she would go with her so they went the same day it's a good thing it was a sunny Mississippi day.

On the ladies journey to see Ms. Jones, Monica mentioned to the native woman that her son will have to wear different clothes to blend in with the other children. She didn't understand at first then she looked around and noticed all the children had on the same clothes she agreed after she asked Monica why are they all dressed like this ? Monica said so no one is different they are all the same when they come to St. Martin's, The native lady liked that idea, they caught up with Ms. Jones.

Monica called for her while running towards her they were both out of breath she tried saying the teachers name again but the native said it instead Monica got her air back she said this is a neighbor she has a son that they would like to have attend your school? Ms. Jones said that she is out of desks, Ms. Jones noticed the native woman's reaction of disappointment Ms. Jones looked at the native woman and said I'll teach him, then Ms. Jones said to Monica I'll need another desk built the ladies bowed and said yes Miss we will see to it.

Days go by so fast and easy things even start to improve around the abandoned ranch that was once called New Beginnings. As far as Leonard's schooling goes his parents think that things are going fine but are they? One day Monica was out for a walk to the little town store for supplies, she also decided to go to St. Martin's school to check on everything. She knocked on the school house, all the children were there but she didn't see Leonard, Ms. Jones came closer to the entrance Monica asked where's Leonard at? She said he is in the closet, she said he has been in there all day.

Monica was getting angry and the teacher sensed this, she went on to say that Leonard puts himself in the closet when he thinks that he did something bad or stupid, but I never punish the children unless they are hurting any of the other children but this is not the case, Ms. Jones did ask if there was something going on at home? Monica said no! He gets sleep as much food as we can afford, bathes, he doesn't work the field yet with his dad he is still a little young, Monica did mention that when the master came to punish the slaves for doing something bad, with the young slaves he would tie them in ropes and put them in small closed door rooms!

Ms. Jones mutters a moaning sigh. Ms. Jones said maybe he would like to feel like he is needed, maybe give him a small job with his father. Monica said I'll give it a shot and Ms. Jones said I'll get Leonard, she said to the native woman bring your son in the morning she also said, I'll need a name for him.

The Native woman bowed as the ladies walked away. As the two ladies walked home, Monica asked when are you going to tell your husband? The native woman just motioned as she was thinking of what to do or say to her husband, Monica whispered do you have a name for him? The native looked up quickly and sternly, while chewing on her nails out of frustration they stopped walking briefly. Monica also said I don't have a name for you either, Monica went on to say if you are going to be neighborly with me, my husband and son, we need to be able to call you something do you have a name pick out for yourself? While still looking at Monica the native woman just motioned no!

While still chewing on her finger nails, Monica said, come on lets go home. We get there slow it will be sun down so they moved on Monica said out loud with some shock thank God we made it home before sun down! To her surprise no one heard. The room was quiet for a moment then Maurice said good thing yous back Mamie gets real dark here in Mercyville Old Mississippi. Monica just said yes dear yours right! The neighbor already went back to her husband, to tell him the news about what the teacher said.

The next morning came, it is a beautiful sunny day not yet snow time but it is Leonard's fifth day of school and also for the parents but Leonard still is not aware of when Monica started to walk then she sees the lady native walking up the path with her son in clothes like Leonard has been wearing, Monica bowed to acknowledge the native lady and so did she, she whispered to Monica call me Sunshine, and my son Sweet Surrender, Monica bowed again then said to the both of them please to meet you, I'm Monica and my sons name is Leonard, then Sunshine bowed and also said please to meet you. Monica said what about your husband Sunshine? Call him Eagle Feather; Monica said my husband is Maurice. Monica said we best get going our boys will be late for school.

As they were walking the boys to the school the boys were following suit by introducing themselves the mothers thought that was so cute but they didn't say anything but they couldn't help but watch them and probably think to themselves why can't life be this nice? Why can't life be this happy? Sunshine said come on children we must walk a little faster as the boys walked faster the mothers looked up to the beautiful light, it was guiding them on their way.

Sunshine whispered to Monica do you see the bright light what is it? Monica said yes! I sees it; it has a beautiful lady in it. Sunshine asked who is she? What does she want? Is she trying to tell us something? Monica was shocked and a bit overwhelmed by these questions all at once, even though Monica saw the light once before and knew the answers she also knew that Sunshine wouldn't understand the answers either, so Monica just said I don't know! The boys made it to school on time but barely, Monica said some loving words to Leonard like mothers always do, gave him a kiss on his cheek and sent him in.

Ms. Jones came to the doorway to receive her new student. Sunshine introduced herself and also Sweet Surrender, Sunshine bent down and spoke to him also with words of encouragement. Sweet Surrender hugged his mother; he had some fear on his face. Sunshine did also but Leonard took Surrenders hand and said come on we'll go together they went in out of Sunshine's sight she got a little nervous, Monica touched her on the shoulder she barely noticed the gesture but Monica said don't worry Sunshine he will be fine! She looked at Monica's eyes and then asked in a whisper can I stay? Can we stay for a minute? I want to stay. Monica knew the feelings she had them too. She said we can stay to listen for a spell. Sunshine got a little closer to the school opening so she can hear better.

Ms. Jones started the class by saying a prayer quietly to herself and then saying to the class we are studying today slavery, Sunshine wanted to react but she didn't. She listened some more then the teacher went on to say all of us and all of the cultures have been slaves and still are today, because if you do not serve Christ, if you are not His obedient servant, you will always be a slave to your sins. Monica hurried to stop Sunshine, she said no!

Sunshine listened a little longer she also whispered be calm it will be okay, the teacher was saying slavery has been known all over the world in many countries some very far away and some not. The teacher said it all started with a country called Norway and then slavery traveled on through the world all the way to here.

This happened to so many different races she went on to say some of you could be slaves or what they call free slaves, maybe some of you know one or are one you will not know and don't not tell we are not here for that, these last words calmed down Sunshine, good thing because Monica was having a hard time holding her down.

This all started because there has always been an overabundance of folk and land but not food, and the land owners needed help because there was always a lot of work that needed to be done, and other countries needed to thin out their people. The teacher went on to say class to make all feel at ease; somehow she knew that Sunshine was still in ear shot. Class we will talk about this subject only to teach you to have respect for others of all kinds of all races. Ms. Jones introduced Sweet Surrender to the class. Sunshine heard all the other children say at once hello to him. This also made Sunshine feel at ease, Monica asked one word softly okay?

The mothers started on their way home to Monica's because she had to make Maurice feel at ease because he has got to be wondering where she is at, they walked for about a mile then the light appeared again but this time the lady came all the way out of the light she was saying something her mouth was moving. Sunshine asked what is she saying? I can't hear her words? Monica decided to get on her knees but she didn't know why Sunshine was confused by this but she did it also out of respect they stayed quiet to try to listen to her words they couldn't take their eyes off the Lady of the Light something kept them still they were like this for a few minutes, the light started to fade, the lady did also. Before she was gone they both got up off their knees and then bowed and watched the light disappear. They went on their way, never to tell anyone.

The mothers both went back to their husbands to see what work still needed to be finished and neither spoke about the light and Sunshine didn't speak about what she heard in Surrenders first class, she did however tell Eagle Feather that she stayed just to make sure Surrender was going to be okay and to tell him about the teacher. Eagle Feather came up the path, after some time went by he addressed Monica and asked if his son was going to come home with the teacher or my son?

She said the teacher Ms. Jones will bring both of them because they live the furthest away and she likes to make sure her kids are safe, Eagle Feather seemed pleased by this he did say also I would like to meet the teacher, then bowed and went back to his work with Maurice, on the plantation. Monica, just sat watching for a spell on the porch just watching

Maurice and Eagle Feather, working together as she sat and thought this is peaceful and how everything is so great for now, and how life is so normal, can life stay this way? Maurice is even happy the crops are doing well. God has been giving us plenty of sun and rain for the seeds to grow. God always seems to know when we need rain or the sun, she thought harvest is coming the children are in school they are learning a lot Maurice and Eagle Feather are working together well. Maurice and I are getting schooling then she wondered for a spell is Surrenders folks going to want schooling also what will they think about us when they find out that we are getting book learning from Ms. Jones?

Before Monica even noticed the time, Ms. Jones was coming up the path. The two boys they are very happy and they are even laughing, Monica thought I have never seen Leonard smile. She thought his smile is so big it made her smile also, Eagle Feather looked up and saw Monica watching the boys come home with the teacher, the two men stopped the work for the day and approached Monica and Eagle Feather asked is that the teacher Monica gestured yes!

She tried to stop him because she wasn't sure what he was going to do, but she decided to give up and watch what he was going to do instead she prayed the whole time that there would not be no trouble and to her surprise there wasn't. Leonard came to see his folks and Surrender meet his mother. At the house Eagle Feather continued talking to Ms. Jones, they bowed at each other then they went their separate ways. Eagle Feather went to his home also with a smile Monica couldn't help but wonder she also wanted to go see Sunshine to get some answers but she changed her mind quickly she still didn't know her neighbors very well.

It is now dinner time all the farm stuff has been put away. Everybody has been cleaned up for dinner the table is even set but Monica still can't help but wonder if things are better for us now, why the light and what would Maurice's reaction be if I told him would he understand? As everyone sat down for supper they said a prayer of thanks,

Maurice asked Leonard is there something on your mind son because you look lost? Leonard responded by saying kind of Father... Monica muttered Oh! What is it? Leonard said mother did you ever notice when Ms. Jones walks me home, she stays for a while then all of the sudden she disappears? Monica was quite taken aback by this question.

She said what do you mean by that? Leonard went on to say she just leaves so fast no one ever sees her leave or she moves faster than a stage coach and horse. Monica thought about this and finally said now that he mentioned it Leonard's right she does leave awfully fast. Monica tried putting that thought out of her head but something keeps bringing her back to it. Monica was going to say something about the lady in the light but Leonard beat her to it, Leonard said mom I have been seeing some kind of light, he said once he saw a lady, he also said that she kind of looks like Ms. Jones, this scared Monica nearly out of her seat.

Maurice just sat there confused about it all; Maurice asked Monica do you know what he means by this? Monica said No! Maurice, this is the first I have heard of it, she had to tell a lie, she felt awful by doing this but she just wasn't sure how her husband would react, but Monica couldn't but wonder what does the lady of the light want, and how come Leonard is also seeing this light and how could the lady be Ms. Jones that couldn't be true then she thought again could this be?

Monica had to put Leonard to bed after his bath. She thought this would be a good time to ask him without his father around about what he has seen with the light, Leonard got into bed after saying a night time prayer. Monica whispered to him a question about the light when do you see the light? He says some times when you are walking me to school and you are looking at the birds as we walk and some times before Ms. Jones comes out of the school to walk me home, Monica asked him one other question did you talk to the lady of the light? He said no! Ma'am nots yet! Monica kissed him good night and went to finish her chores for the day, she continued to wonder what does it all mean, and then she heard a voice you need to go to church tomorrow! She looked around to see who said it but how without Maurice, tomorrow is Saturday? Monica asked Maurice if she can go into town tomorrow before he answered she said I would like to see some of the town to see some of the people if that be okay with you? Maurice said after some thought sure Mamie yous can go I stills have work in the fields to do, she said thanks honey I am most grateful, Maurice asked are you taking Leonard? Monica said I will if you wish it, he said please take him I'll be in the fields all day, she said that would be fine honey, Even though she was secretly smiling inside but she dare not tell Maurice about wanting to go find a church to pray in or even seeing the light. Monica remembered what her son said Ms. Jones mentioned to him that the church with the same name to his school was just down the road, he also mentioned the teacher also said it was an abouts a mile from school.

The following morning arrives; Monica couldn't get out of bed fast for her taste. She wanted to hurry and get breakfast on the table and get Leonard up to greet the new day and of course she so wanted to go pray the day away if she could, when the table was cleared and Maurice went out to start the fields for the day, Monica got her and Leonard ready for their day as well she did hear Maurice say where's Eagle Feather today? Monica didn't pay much attention she wanted to go see God, but she had to find His home first Monica said to Maurice we are going he waved as to say okay! Bye! Monica asked Leonard what was the way to the church? What did you teacher say? So he repeated his words miles from the school. She thought it out and said sos we will pretend to go to your school because it's on the way, as they got to the school there was a light on which was odd because Leonard said teacher doesn't work on the weekends, but why then is there a light on?

They both approached the door way one looked in the other saw a light beaming in the pathway to where they need to go to find the church, Monica looked in and said huh that is strange there is no one here but who left the candle burning for light to see by? Leonard tugged on her dress and said momma what is that light in front of me?

Monica turned around barely hearing what he just asked, she said huh? Leonard pointed up then she looked up in shock he continued to watch the light and Monica heard a voice coming from the light: a lady, she tried to listen a little harder because it was so low, Monica finally heard Monica, God is watching over you and your family, she said your friends and your family will always be labeled as slaves because of the law won't change, she wanted to say something to this but something or someone stopped her, I need you to go pray. Then Leonard finally heard something coming from the light. He heard Leonard I will always be with you, I will always be watching over you no matter your age. God loves you. I need you to help your mother find church. The voice asked Leonard, can you do this Leonard, he said uh huh out of fear. The Lady in the Light said to Leonard in a whisper remember, always remember then it was gone.

They both continued on their journey to find this church Leonard followed the path Ms. Jones taught him and there it is, St. Martin Roman Catholic Church: names the same way as the school. Monica open the large wood door and held it for Leonard to go in first, then when she went in she looked around and she just couldn't drink all the beautiful art in, it is all over the ceilings and the images on the walls, all she could whisper was wow! Leonard saw someone familiar, he tried to gently pull his mother but she just couldn't stop staring at all the paintings and building design, she did however make her eyes come down and she finally discovered that her neighbors were already there. Monica finally remembered what Maurice said there is no Eagle Feather today Monica was slightly shocked, she didn't know Indians went to church. She finally saw a man dressed more differently than everyone else, she stopped him and asked him a question about Ms. Jones, he introduced himself as Father Matthias, and he finally said Ms. Jones! He said after some thought I don't know of anyone then he thought again and said well there was one but he said that is impossible for it to be her. Monica asked why? He said she has been dead for ten years, Monica had no idea what to think do or say to that so she just said thank you father I will keeps asking around, she was so confused by his words she had no idea what to think.

Monica went back to the neighbors and sat next to Sunshine. Before Monica could tell Sunshine what she just heard Sunshine whispered words like a message, Sunshine Don't Worry God Will Always Fill in the Blanks! God Will Always Show Us The Way! If Monica wasn't confused before, she is now. She whispered to herself what does that mean? She sat down next to her son in a long silence while looking up at this huge cross with a man dead hanging from it.

Then the door open fast and loudly everyone looked up and to Monica's surprise it was Maurice, he was going to ask what are you doing here but everyone shushed him he sat down next to Monica he was going to ask in a loud whisper but he got shushed again sat there and then he noticed the dead man on the cross. He just kept looking at it he couldn't take his eye off it.

Quite many years have gone by since all of this happened Monica, Maurice, and the neighbors are all passed now it is just the boys Leonard and Sweet Surrender but they are still going to church like there folks did all the time every Sunday, until God called them home but the boys do take heart in there was never anyone looking for either families because they were still labeled as slaves not free, The year is now 1899 Leonard is still in

Mercyville Miss. He is married to a woman with the same blue eyes that he has and they also had a couple of sons with the same blue eyes, Leonard continued working the farm his daddy was working and doing very well for hisself, he is also a Deacon for St. Martins church and Sweet Surrender became a Pharmacist before he became a priest Father Surrender, but he doesn't get back to Mercyville very often but when he does he pops in on the young Moses family, and as for Ms. Jones yes! Leonard and surrender discovered that she is a ghost but they never did tell their parents, every time Monica brought up the subject Leonard always said God Will Always Fill in the Blanks! God Will Always Show Us The Way! Leonard always sees her still teaching other free slave children of all races but he will never tell anyone her secret.

THE GRAVE DIGGER

BY BERNADINE MISURA
(9-19-06)

Who is this grave digger, who is she? Why do they call her this? I said I don't know her name, but I know she is very pretty, and very lonely, she goes through life as an unknown.

Where no one knows her or what she really does, but I do know she gives her love to others, even to you. Then when they receive what they want of her, they either run or go away without as much as a thank you for everything you do for me.

She is a very caring and giving person no matter what. She will help you, yes, even to your grave, but not without love and honor so you may have everlasting peace, she will give her life for you. Know this to be true, but does anyone say thank you? No! She goes happily on with her work, for the Lord.

When she has to bury one of her own such as: a family member or her treasured pet, does anyone go comfort her? No! Does she show or feel pain? Yes I'm sure she does, she quietly prays to God every day, so her cares will be washed away, merrily, carries on, when you don't want to handle something people go to the grave digger, she won't mind, she just smiles and brightens your day.

She always brightens my way. How do I know this? Because the grave digger is me, I am she, the secret is to love and serve our Lord, become one of his Vessels, it is written that you will never die; you want to give it a try? Such as I. Come with me I will help you.

THE HOLY WETNESS OF GOD

BY BERNADINE ZIEGLER
(6/6/15)

His Holy Wetness, what is His Holy Wetness? Well it is the Holy Water used in the church: God's House, what does this mean? Is there something you have to do to receive it? All you have to do is show up to His House and do the sign of the cross with the Holy Water in the font, after you do receive it, will you feel differently? Yes! I always feel better: I feel more at peace and any cares or worries I may have get lost in His Holy House They just seem to get chased away I feel totally cleansed. May the Lord bless me!

What is this Holy Wetness made of? You know that is really a good question: because I have wondered this myself but too afraid to mention, I have done some checking on this question: the answer to the question is wine, ash, and salt, the blessing water for babies is made of oil and Catechumens and Holy Chrism, plain water is used for the baptism because John the Baptist did the same by just water in the river Jordan.

There was a day not long ago that God asked me to take some of the Holy Water and disburse it on to a building of evil while praying all evil away so His unborn babies take their first breath live and enjoy all of God's World, and for evil take its final rest which will be best, I did do as He asked of me, but I did also commit some crimes on the Great Thee which is He, I did a foolish thing I did not put my complete trust in Him I did not have complete faith in what He had asked of me, I also let fear of evil over take me shame on me. May the Lord forgive me!

I finished my task and went home with no recourse from anyone if I just would of put my complete faith, and trust in Him I would have had more fun, a few weeks go by and to my surprise my husband told me about an article that read abortions are down and I also heard on this day that the Pro-Lifers got a bunch of tough laws passed that make it impossible for anyone to have an abortion, when I heard and read the news I was amazed by the true wills of God and I will make this vow to the Holy One, I will never have any doubt, or fear, I will have complete faith, trust in the Lord always!

So when the mass has Holy Water sprinkled upon you always remember that this is a true blessing, and when you are sprinkled with the Holy Wetness you become a Holy Witness to His awesome love for us all. So when the Lord asks you to do something don't ask questions just do as He asks it is that easy, Be His Holy Witness to His Holy Wetness, at least let's do it for His children that would be all of us, there is really no more to mention. Except May the Lord have mercy on us all.

THE HUMBLE TRAVELER

BY BERNADINE MISURA
IN 2001

There is a traveler who does his destination know
Moment by moment like a step by step, he lives
His journey slowly, but surely steadily,

His pace, tells of no hurry his countenance carries
No cries and his demeanor
depicts no pain, his life
Style follows no lavishness, clothed by a touching
Humility.

He has met some flops, and hops, and through jars,
And jolts, and jounces, too.

By leaps and bounds, bumps and bruises, and some
Bounces, but it's all a foot in the ride and rhyme, agait,
A pace, a dance, of life and the humble traveler journeys
On.

THE LAST BOOK ON EARTH

BY BERNADINE ZIEGLER

(11-27-13)

The year is 3026 A.D. My name is Jocelyn, I am 9 years of age, and it is just my dad and I. My mother passed away a few years back. I do miss her a lot after all I am 9, and a girl needs to have her mother around for the female years, at least that is what my aunt tells me, her name is Elizabeth. I go and see her every day after school. My dad's name is Michael, and he is the sheriff of the small town of Trinity, Ca. where we live. The town is so small everyone knows everyone else and there are no large bad crimes just some small ones like stealing food or clothes.

My dad lets me walk the neighborhood when I don't have school, so I walked down to the craft store, I always loved it in there just me and my mom Kate. We always looked at the new crafts to sew; she sewed all the time and she taught me too. I kept looking at the bird crafts, I always remember how much she loved hearing the birds in the morning, she even took pictures and sewed some pictures and hung them on the walls, just seeing them makes me smile, and I truly miss her.

When I stopped looking at the pictures of birds I looked up and there is a very tall man standing in front of me, he has kind of long hair for a man, it is curly and lays on his very large shoulders, his eyes are brown just like his hair, but he has the funniest ears I never did see before, I only saw those kind of ears on a character in one of my books my mom used to read to me. He was motioning me over to him and calling my name, I don't know what to do, I look around for help and no one seems to see or hear him, I am a little scared, but I do go over to him, he is holding a very heavy looking book it is all white and very thick, he is holding it with both of his hands.

The man said his name is Kieran, he said that he is in charge of the book and that he needs a helper and he asked me if I would like to help him? I don't understand, I am just a kid what can I do? He said come with me my child. I didn't want to but something told me to. He went into the back of the store there is a safe, he opened it and held the book again he said, Jocelyn, I need you to guard this book, he got down to my level and asked me again if I would watch over his book, he proceeded to lock the safe and said to me if anything happens, I need to grab the book and take it with me. He said again Jocelyn, will you do this for me? I said I don't understand but I will do as you ask. He got down to my size again touched my shoulders smiled at me. His brown eyes were gleaming with light, he said thank you.

Now I must go and help the others he said while still smiling at me, he was making me very nervous. He asked me are you going to be okay? Before I could answer his smile got larger and brighter with the light, he said don't worry Jocelyn you'll be fine, he said again everything will be okay! If you ever need me just call my name can you remember? I said his name he said that is right, he said now I really must go. We both turned away but I turned back around the man was gone.

I left the Trinity Craft Store; I went to find my father. I found my dad at work; he asked are we ready to go home? I shook my head yes, he asked did you have fun today? I answered yes! But for some reason I didn't tell him about all of my day, I guess he would think it is a silly kids story that I was making up, so I didn't tell him, but I did tell him about the pretty pictures of the birds I saw. He smiled and told me to wash for dinner. My father and I were eating dinner, it got quiet I said dad do you know a man named Kieran, he is tall, dark haired, gleaming eyes and has really strange ears? He kind of laughed and said no! No one I know why do you ask? I said he is a stranger I saw in the store today. My dad is the town sheriff so he would know, but I did not dare to tell anymore. Dad did say after dinner get a bath we have church in the morning, I said quietly as I left the table yes father.

It's the next morning the sun is shining bright I always love Sundays and going to church, mommy always put me in dresses and hats she said proper ladies wore dresses and young ladies wore hats to church. I loved going with mom, she had a smile that would light up the church, then she would smile at me while holding my hand, mom always loved to hear the words of God and so does my dad. My dad and I go to sit down. I look around and say the church is full today, no response but that didn't matter. I looked up when the priest went up to the podium to speak the blessed words of Christ, I couldn't help it but I kept staring at him. He looks just like the man yesterday, but the priest's ears are normal, everything else is the same, the priest looks at me and smiled and his eyes are still gleaming with the light.

After I came home I changed my clothes and hung up my churching clothes, then I went out to play with my friends. It's a sunny June day, the birds are singing, and it's another year without my mother. A year has gone by now since I last spoke with Kieran, I haven't seen or heard from him and the book, his book, is still in the safe where he placed it and locked it. I can't help but wonder what is so special about this book. And why does he need me to guard it? What is it all about, who is it all about, and who wrote it? I was playing tag with my friends and they stopped. One of them said did anyone feel that? No answer we played some more and it got stronger. I shouted it's a tremor! There was a lot of shouting and kids were running home for cover.

I heard my dad calling, Jocelyn! Get home for cover then he shouted everyone get to safety get covered. I got in the house and ran for the tub, dad grabbed a mattress and jumped in and pulled the mattress over us. It seemed like hours while the tremors were going, then there was nothing but silence, it was torture to hear nothing, dad and I got out of the tub and we went outside and noticed our house's roof is gone but the house can be fixed, dad said. Then I looked further around the town with dad holding my hand, the town of Trinity is all gone as far as the eye can see. It is all rubble and white dust everywhere.

I don't see anyone else yet, we stood and looked around for a few minutes and dad finally said, come on Jocelyn, and we must search for others. Dad got down to my level and said I need your help to look for any living breathing thing, people and animals, can you do that for me Jocelyn? I wanted to cry because we may be the only ones, but I said yes! Father. I asked what about the church did it make it through, is it okay? I asked do you think there is anyone else? He said I don't know all we can do is pray now. I said can we? May we pray for the others? He answered with tears in his eyes yes! So we did I always had mom's and my rosary with me and dad always kept his on him, we said the rosary prayer for everyone.

Just before we started to walk in different directions to find any survivors, I looked behind me and the man named Kieran was back. He smiled at me while bowing down he said Jocelyn do you remember me? I just kept looking at his ears. He also asked how is my book? His ears are back and so is the gleam in his eyes. I said we are going to find others that might be alive. I said your book is still in the safe. He got down to my level and told me he is the Leprechaun King, I have abilities to change my appearance when needed, he went on to say that his work is with the church and God, but he also said the church is fine everyone made it through okay, but we must retrieve the book, then he changed back when he was speaking to my father.

He said while still looking at me God told me to seek you out so we can help each other, he said to my dad the church took on some damage but it is fixable, he asked me again how is the book? I still didn't answer, he said to my dad I am here to help you find the others and there are other survivors. He changed his clothes before my eyes he is now in priestly attire there is even a cross on his robes, it is beautiful he couldn't help but smile and he said come we must get the book and then find the others.

We went behind the craft store some of it is still there and so is the safe. Kieran opened it, he reached in and with some delight the book came out just as good as he put it in there, he got down to my size again smiled and said you did a good job thank you now we must go. He stood up holding the book with his two hands and said if anything ever happened to this book everything would cease to exist, because the book is God's book and his words. He held the book above his head while we were walking to find survivors the first person we found was my teacher Miss Haley, then we found some dogs and cats, we walked some more then we found the kids I was playing with they made it we kept walking and found more on the way and the line behind the priest kept growing and growing.

My teacher told us in school this stuff always happens in Ca. but this is the first time I ever experienced it. I always wondered how did they ever carry on from all the rubble but now I can answer this question for myself somehow you just do, his name is God, and with the help of the good father, so I say God bless to them and to us the survivors. It is the year 3027 a beautiful day in June the sun is shining and we all still have our health and our church there is no other wealth, we must all carry on and love one another no matter the situation.

.

THE LONE ANGEL FEATHER

BY BERNADINE ZIEGLER
(4/23/15)

The lone angel feather came to me in a unusual way, one my worries was getting to me and I went outside to look up to the sky and pray to God and ask him why, why am I always supposed to be the strong one? Why did you choose me? I continued to pray to Him, it seemed like hours. I begged Him, Lord Help my husband and I be free of all our financial difficulties. Please don't let us become destitute. I continued to say please Lord I know not what to do help me please.

Some more time went by I just couldn't stop looking up into the sky, it seemed like the sunlight got brighter even though I had no idea if He heard me or listened to me. Yes! I did wonder if He even cared. If so then why do I constantly have all of this despair at times it seems like it gets out of control; I asked the Lord please tell me what to do how can I make my life better; guide me, show me, help me be strong, Lord I am weak take my life from me! I can't get out of this financial mess, I just couldn't help but wonder does He really hear me?

A lot of time went by for some reason; I wondered why my husband didn't come out and check on me, but I was okay with it so I continued to speak to the Lord. At times I thought I heard Him but I just really wasn't sure but I still prayed for a very long time, it seemed like all day. I am sure He is tired of hearing from me; tired of all my troubles but who else can I talk to, who else will hear me, who else can I release all of my fears and cares of this world who else?

A couple of days go by I still have all my troubles and many trials and tribulations, but I feel a little lighter, like some weight is off my shoulder.

I opened the back door to my car I saw on the back seat a single white feather. I couldn't stop looking at it, where did it come from? What is it made of? I went through everything I don't have any goose down stuff and I haven't been in the car for days, so how did it get in there?

Then I saw an image of an angel and she was trying to show me where it came from off of her winged shoulder. There were some missing feathers but she wasn't hurt. She was mouthing the words the Lord Hears and Cares for you she also motioned that He Loves you and wanted you to have this one lone angel feather so you know you will always have His Love.

THE PROCLAMATION

BY BERNADINE ZIEGLER
(2-21-13)

My dearest one: ever since God helped us find each other, I knew we were destined to be together. I could feel nothing but Love from Above telling me this is the man who is going to marry me. I couldn't help the feeling of finally being free to love and be loved, a sudden glee came over me, what could this feeling be?

I did not know if my feelings were true: then I looked into your eyes, I realized I can't hear the man's voice that has been calling me for many years now, I know it's true you are for me and I am for you, I claim you as my choice forever and a day in any kind of way. May this be God's Perfect Day?

My dearest one I make this proclamation to you, when we get married our love will always take us on an adventure and it will always be a new yes! We'll fight, we'll still love each other in spite and we will burn up the night with Eternal Light, let's light the flame, our lives will never be the same.

When we do argue: how about we look into each other's eyes and say these words, my love ever so dear we must remember that the Eternal Light brought us together so we can walk through any kind of marriage weather by saying you will always have my heart it will never fall apart, you are in my soul, you have my ever burning love, I promise you that we'll never become cold embers.

THE RESCUER

BY BERNADINE MISURA
(8-26-06)

The rescuer, who is she, do I know her? Who can she be? I stood silently by thinking it is I. I did hear that she was bitten when she was thirteen years of age. No one around to help her but somehow she got the help she needed, there was three dogs on her and she just walks away, just like it's just another day. A neighbor lady said it sounds like you know who she is, yes! I watched everything happen, I don't know her name but I saw the torture and pain. I so wanted to say hey it's me, I'm the one all the buzz is about.

Everybody is saying it was the Good Lord, who saved her and gave her a gift, I heard a sigh o' what kind of gift? She can communicate with all God's critters, like dogs, and cats, I heard she even saved many of his treasured birds, and bugs, she even believes in saving snakes, she doesn't like them but she considers them all God's creatures and they have a right to live, I had to stay silent so no one found me out, but inside I'm doing the twist and jig.

I even heard talk around the streets I hear the rescuer saved another girl from the rapist, who is she? They looked at me I answered; I don't know, but I wish I could join in her show! Some of the petty criminals said I think she is even responsible for getting my friends arrested, I thought to myself, thank God they think nothing of me because of my epilepsy, I pray to God that they never figure me out, that the old neighborhood never figured that it was me all along.

I am the rescuer they are talking about. But the Good Lord is my rescuer, He doesn't mind if He is found out as for me, I'll keep doing it secretly, my name is Bernadine. I am the rescuer and I am also the head of the crime crusaders. God will always be my rescuer.

THE SINFUL SOCK

BY BERNADINE ZIEGLER
(2/11/15)

The sinful sock, the sorrowful sock. This term is new to me. What does this mean? I am going to make a guess a sinful sock is another way of saying unholy and that would be sorrowful wouldn't it? But doesn't everyone prefer the unholy sock? And the holy sock everyone throws away but if the sock is holy then isn't it sinless, it makes one wonder doesn't it?

The sinful sock yes, it is sorrowful or is it, it can be worn more because it isn't torn but since it is unholy wouldn't that be sorrowful, to the wearer and the one that is holy gets tossed out to the trash so wouldn't that make it sorrowful also, but to the barer when one is holy is it a sin to toss it out? Well, what are you going to do? I will choose hmm oh! What do I do Oh! However do I figure this out?

The next time you look at your socks what one will you choose? When one sock is holy and one sock is not what are you going to do? Will you toss out the holy one and find another mate that is unholy or will you toss them both out because you can't make a choice or is it because you have no voice? However will you decide how to make things right?

THE SUN

BY BERNADINE ZIEGLER
(1-28-11)

Come back sun, let this cold be done and gone, so I can say to everyone come on let's have some fun maybe until dawn. Sun, sun, where have you gone? Sun, sun, you are so perfect and round, how do I know if you are even upside down?

Sun, sun, oh how you burn so bright you help us on Earth, to tell us the difference between day and night, without your warmth it gives me such a fright. As for the cool and light of the moon, I can't do without you. I wouldn't know what to do without you.

Come back sun, my stress level is becoming so worn and undone I yearn for your warmth on a beautiful June, summer morn. could you bring some rain so it can stop the pain. Please God, bring back the sun soon for this I pray so I can relax and play all day. I beg this of you Lord, please say okay.

THE TRICKLING, TRICKLING WATER

BY BERNADINE ZIEGLER
(3-21-11)

The trickling, trickling slow moving water,
for somereason all I can do is stand here
and watch it flow so slowly, slowly;
just look at it go.

Where does it come from where does it go?
As Istand here I wonder will I ever know,
but oh whata show.

There is only one that knows where the trickling
trickling water comes from where it goes and when
the time comes God will let you know when he
will stop his slow trickling, trickling water from its
slow moving flow.

HOW TO PRAY THE ROSARY

BY BERNADINE ZIEGLER

(2/25/15)

How to pray The Holy Rosary just the way the Lord taught me: You start out the same way by saying the Apostles Creed, and the one Our Father at the beginning, and the three Hail Mary's, and the Glory Be, it becomes different when you start the First Mysteries, instead of saying one for every ten set of beads, the Lord wants all of the Mysteries said together on the same set of ten beads, then the Hail Mary's, Glory Be's. Since the Good Lord taught me how to pray the Rosary, it couldn't be wrong! Right? Oh! I'm sure the Holy Mother didn't want the rosary said the way it is today, all divided up simple because it never gets finished, and people either get bored or lose their place, the Lord God doesn't like this at all. However we still pray on Saturdays for the Holy Mother, The Joyful Mysteries, After all the Holy Rosary is Hers, and the Joyful Mysteries is Her main part.

Then for the second set of ten beads: you say all together the Mysteries of Light, repeat the Hail Mary's Glory Be's and Our Father as normal then on the next set of ten beads: all of the Sorrowful Mysteries, no split up, no divisions, on the fourth set of ten beads: The Glorious Mysteries, you are probably wondering what to do with the last set of ten beads? Well the Lord said on the last ten set say prayers for all of his other children living and the dead. After I prayed the rosary as He taught me on several occasions, I have seen the doors to Heaven open up. Angels came for a look to see who is praying to the Lord as He commanded.

Then when you come to the medal in the middle this is always for the Prayer Hail Holy Queen: and then the prayer that goes with the Holy Rosary, I will write it out because I don't think to many people know

about it, the prayer is LET US PRAY. O GOD , WHOSE ONLY BE-
GOTTEN SON, BY HIS LIFE, DEATH AND RESURRECTION,
HAS PURCHASED FOR US THE REWARDS OF ETERNAL
LIFE , GRANT, WE BESEECH YOU, THAT WE WHO MED-
ITATE ON THESE MYSTERIES OF THE MOST HOLY RO-
SARY OF THE BLESSED VIRGIN MARY, MAY BOTH IMITATE
WHAT THEY CONTAIN AND OBTAIN WHAT THEY PROM-
ISE, THROUGH THE SAME CHRIST OUR LORD. AMEN.

Before I put my rosary down I continue praying all of the prayers on
the back of the church Missal, well there you have it: the reason why
the Lord wanted it said this way is because he asked why are the Mysteries of His Life split up? He lived all of these all at once not split up
on different days of the week. He is not saying the way it has been done
for several centuries is wrong oh! He just doesn't understand the division of days and the division of His Living Mysteries. After I taught my
husband the true way of the Holy Rosary he said there was like an inner
peace that came over him and the feeling of wanting to do more for the
Lord, my husband's reaction was truly amazing to me. The Lord also
said that He wants me to teach others including His priests. I said My
Lord I will do as you ask but how do I get your Priests to change their
ways? He answered by saying don't worry my daughter have courage
I'll be with you at all times, I must admit I'm still very scared but I am
also aware that the church His Church needs to be corrected.

THE VOICE OF GOD

BY BERNADINE ZIEGLER
(2-18-13)

The voice of God comes in so many forms such as God himself, 1 of the many prophets, and his many vessels of the past. For instance such as Elijah, Noah, Moses, David, John the Baptist, Mary's husband Joseph, who said yes! God I will raise your son as my own and give him a place to roam, I know this man gave everything he could. Does he ever get honorable mention? No! But I think he should.

And of course Jesus God's Son, and our first priest, without him we wouldn't have a past or a present. I saved the best for last His Mother Holy Mary Mother of the Ultimate one, there are so many to be named such as the twelve chosen to start his Holy Reign.

St. Peter, the builder and keeper of his first holy church and now the keeper of the pearly gates he now shows you your fate. Now there are the Epistles and the Church Missals, or you may know as the Scriptures, the New and Old Testament it really doesn't matter they're all the same they are all found in the Holy Bible and in there it bares every ones name, it doesn't matter who spoke or wrote them they are all his sacred words, they are all the Voice of God.

Today he has many vessels on his great earth who speak of his Holy Words, I know I go to see one every Sunday, when the Holy church bells ring, they are calling, come children, come all heed my call! When I go to see Jesus on the cross who died for us all and became our Holy King, and to hear the alter bells ring as God's Voice, and say yes! I accept the blessing of the Eucharistic Bread, so you may receive a piece of my Manna today in my stead.

How can I get all of you to understand the Voice of God, it can be seen and heard everywhere because God created everything including the grass you stand on and the rain? Don't you see God is love and that is what he promises us all. So why don't we all stand and say God please take my hand catch me when I may fall. Will you ever see that he always watches over you and me, yes!

He gave us our own voice and our own choice, lets all extend our hands and ask God to help us understand and to take us with him to the Promised Land. What is your choice? Hear my voice pray to God and say here I am Lord, I ask where are you?

THERE'S SOMETHING ABOUT THOSE WEDNESDAYS

BY BERNADINE MISURA
(10-5-06)

It seems like odd things always happened to me, on a certain day of the week, it started when I was very young, I wasn't aware that these things kept going on for some reason it was always on a Wednesday, as I got a little older I became more aware of these odd happenings. Every Wednesday there was always something different and for a long time they just happened to me, directly; why me I don't know will I ever know?

Don't get me wrong some of these thing weren't all bad there was some good too, I never know what to expect when Wednesday comes I never knew what to do, as I got older like in my teens, I was getting ready for my high school graduation, I asked God, why, what is it about these Wednesdays, he said I'm testing you! I asked him testing me Lord may I ask why?

Please forgive me lord but I don't understand, I'm not complaining lord, I'm just wondering did I do something wrong? Am I being tested, because I need to prove I am devoted to you? I get a feeling I got on his nerve because the test got a lot harder, and the happenings on Wednesdays got more odd and now they are not happening directly to me they are happening around me even with my family.

I was watching a religious show one night about a saint and of her plight in her life and something hit me, her experiences became mine all of these things happened to her on the same days, just about in the same way on Wednesdays, she even died on a Wednesday, in all my born days, I don't think I could have been able to figure it out if it wasn't for God, but this one saint is one of many but I know she's the one.

I have discovered there has been other saints just like this particular one, who has had similar plights in life. Have I passed the tests of God? I pray yes! But I also pray that the Lord won't stop testing me because He wouldn't love me.

THERE'S SO MUCH SNOW

BY BERNADINE ZIEGLER

(1-15-11)

There's so much snow out here I can't even compare, I'm not going to try or dare, all I can do is stand here and stare, What am I going to do with all of this, my driveway is such a mess! Somehow I will have to shovel all of this somewhere, but to where? There is so much snow out here there's no way to see a road, everything is so white, if I was a kid I would be shouting with delight.

There is not one spot that the hand of Jack Frost missed, everything is caught up in the snows abyss, my frost bite is now in distress, shoveling the drive, I still need to finish, somehow I need to work it out. I often think, oh what a year this is going to be. Wild and free but not for me.

Where did all of this snow come from, and where is it all going to go? Right now I would rather go someplace warm, so my legs, arms, muscles have no strain or pain, and frost bite don't become cold, or worn, and torn. Oh please God make it go away maybe for a day, I would rather play than shovel all day. Please say okay! If is no, I still will love you even as I dig through all of this snow, there's so much snow, I think it is because to many people told the Good Lord No!

TODExY

WRITTEN BY BERNADINE MISURA
ON 6-2-07

Today I am happy to take you as my lawful wedded husband, but before this day you have stood by my side and gave my whole world new meaning, you have already showed me a great love I thought I was going to go without, then God pointed you out to me, and now someone loves me, can you see me beaming? I love you.

Today this is the day I say I do to you, I can't help but think how will my life be like when I Become your wife? Have you thought about how you will feel when you become my husband, I know we don't make a lot of money, no that's not funny, with God's will I know we will some how make it still. I know we will.

Today is our beautiful wedding that we are going to give to our Lord and maybe open up Heavens Door at least a little more than before, to get married in the eyes of the Lord, and He and His Angels as our witness, and I guess, our wedding will always be the best, God, is the reason why we will do well, and to ask him why he will never tell.

TRANSFORMATION

⌒⌒

BY BERNADINE MISURA
(1-31-00)

This story starts in the country of Australia, in a small town called Burden Town also known as turn right city, located somewhere in the middle of the continent, this is where I currently live my name is Kathy Shear Reese, I live and co-own a one hundred acre farm with my father Clifford Reese, the year is 1837 it is a Tuesday, my dad and I wanted a nice quite place for my mother to spend the rest of her days in peace she sadly isn't with us anymore she lost her battle of breast cancer a couple of years ago, the farm cost fifty cents an acre kind of expensive at the time.

My man friend visits me a lot and he also helps out with the farm his name is Joseph, he and my father get along fine my father keeps praying some soon Joseph will ask me to marry him and just a couple of months ago we encountered a stranger a drifter one day he knocked on our door tipped his hat and he asked me if he could stay with us for a while?

He said I will be glad to work your farm for my keep I was always taught to welcome folks in for some food and shelter because you never know if someday you may need help, his name is Gideon, he said I come from Perth Australia, I came here because I need to get away from my current life which includes his six brothers, and fined a new life on his own and for his own in his many travels he stopped at my farm and diner and never looked back. Me and dad are grateful to Gideon and Joseph my fiancée for their help because dad is getting to old and is unable to run the farm himself, sometime soon Joseph and I are going to tell father the good news but not now.

It was dinner time and everybody but Gideon is in the house he is still harvesting some of the crops, I was about to call Gideon for supper I looked out the window and that is when I saw him running towards the house I kept looking to see what is making him scram towards the house but all I could see was a mild wind I quickly opened the door to let him in.

When Gideon came in he was out of breath he was trying to catch his breath but all I could do was to ask him what is a matter he finally said after a few minutes time and said look out the window again, Clifford was the first one this time at the window, Clifford and Gideon said at the same time there is a very bad storm coming our way Gideon continued on saying to me all the farm is bounded and tied down I saw it coming before the storm formed.

Joseph got out of his chair to look outside he didn't believe that a storm was just going to pop up and have that kind of strength I was with him looking out I whispered to Joseph I'm scared he whispered back and rubbed my shoulder he said don't worry by God's Will we will all be fine Joseph saw I wanted to cry but I just couldn't he held me tight, Gideon said we must hurry for cover we have no time to prepare.

Clifford was sitting on the on the day bed in the living room his favorite place to relax and watch the world gone by, he said I don't know what you all are afraid of it's just a wind storm he said with a slight chuckle, the three of us looked at him out of shock and said what do you mean?

No one ever believes my dad he is not too smart when it comes to weather problems, Clifford never answered Kathy's question not because he's rude because he just disappeared, I said quite loudly like a scream I said Joseph, Gideon, where is he they glanced to see then we all realized that it just was my dad missing but everything was gone in fact the whole town was gone or is it that Kathy, Joseph, and Gideon are the ones that disappeared, somehow the three ended up in a town called Wearington Ohio nicknamed Enticement in the year 1951 on a Friday.

When they found out where they were they didn't seem scared for some reason they just seemed confused like they belonged somewhere else but they couldn't remember where Gideon said does anyone feel strange like they just went through a different time lapse Joseph said is everyone all right then he got up from where he was, Joseph walked over to me and Gideon and Kathy and asked out loud what was that where are we?

I said I'm fine I think I'm not sure but are we who we were before I mean am I still Kathy are you still Gideon and are you still Joseph my fiancée we all said at the same time I think so. All three of them asked where we just came from can anyone remember, they all said no! I asked who are what brought us here and why? Gideon said all I can remember is a storm then he looked at Joseph he motioned his hands like he didn't know either. Joseph finally said after some time we had better go find out where we are at least see how the other folk live here where ever here is, or what are placing in life here will be.

When they went to go see the town of Wearington, and maybe to whoever sent them they have to find their new place in life, all three of them decided to stay together in case this may happen again they went to go look at the town and I myself found out that I own a town diner not a large diner it is kind of small it is connected to my white house they are on an acre of land I have no kids Gideon, Joseph, and I are all still single Gideon is still working on the neighborhood farms as a harvester, Joseph is a business attorney, I did notice that there are a lot of folks walking down the sidewalks.

There are a lot of four wheeled machines that go bye as well they go in two directions I think they are called cars but I'm not sure they do have a nice smooth road to travel on not like the horse buggies on the dirt roads that I think I came from, all I know that everything is so very different from what I am thinking, the guys came into the diner to talk about their discovery's I asked have we been transformed somehow they both answered I don't know, but why us? Gideon said I read somewhere that Gideon was a judge for Christ and Joseph is the step father of Jesus I said well what about me Kathy or my birth name Katherine?

Gideon answered there are some many saint Katherine's I said do you think it was God that brought us here before the guys could answer I leaned in and said why our we here what is here He would be worried about and why us? The guys said we will have to be patient and wait for the Lords Orders we are supposed to be His servants, so I said you think it was Him so we are a part of a transformation or is it a transfiguration I responded by saying I guess you're right all we can do is wait but can we three wait together for His Word, we are all in agreement.

I went outside after closing down the diner for the night, me and the guys were standing in front of the diner on the porch there are three white rocking chairs but we didn't sit in them, we watched the sky then we all saw the lights go up to the sky at really fast speed then we heard a popping noise from the same lights, I looked around and saw there are a lot of folks out here Gideon was about to sit down so he could watch the rest of the show sitting down but before he did he asked a passer bye he motioned to a man and said excuse me kind sir could you tell me what day is it? The man smiled and said it's the 4th of July 1980 Gideon motioned as to say thank you but I said to the man kind sir may I ask you a question if you please? The man lifted his hat off his head and said sure thing miss, where is this place and what is it called?

The gentleman said Worrysville Ohio, and before the other man asks me it's 7:30 at night, then I curtsied and said thank you kind sir, Gideon

Joseph, and I sat down I said did something happen to us again but this time the town looks the same but the name and year has changed I am so confused before I could ask why Gideon said does any of you remember your Bible we all said yes!

Let's think this out I remember a cloud a storm Joseph said I remember the year 1837 the year of pope Leo 12th and I said weren't we just in the year 1951 before the fireworks Gideon said pope Pius the 11th and now it's the year 1980 the year of pope John Paul the 2nd then Joseph finally said I am the same Joseph that is the step father of Jesus and is married to the Holy Mother of God and Gideon said and I am here on God's order also because I am not just a judge for Him I am known as the punisher of soldiers we both are helpers of Christ and we are here to see if you're worthy of the same gifts as we have been given by God, I said wait is this a dream or is this real am I being tested is that why every time we changed places are names and faces never changed but the places did these were all places where poor and people of need live and if I remember rightly Gideon gave to the hungry and so did Joseph because that is the Jewish way and I am being tested to see if I would give of everything I have to the poor I asked am I right?

Both of the guys said we are shocked you didn't catch on when we mentioned the importance of our names, I asked them both so am I doing right by God what is your judgment Gideon what do you think Joseph? They both said you are doing very well just keep The Lords Laws and keep His Word, always believe in Him He loves you that is why he sent us both. I said I will love Him forever then my world as I know it went back to normal.

MY VISIONS OF IRELAND

BY MARK E. ZIEGLER

I WAS BORN PART IRISH AND I HAD THIS VISION AT THE AGE OF 52. THE ROCK OF CASHEL HAD A STRONG IMPACT ON ME. I HAVE ALSO HAD A VISION OF A ROAD THAT GOES IN A WINDING DIRECTION, PEACEFUL ENOUGH FOR A STROLL ON A BEAUTIFUL SUMMER DAY. I EVEN SAW ONE OF THE MANY FARM FOLK PULLING HIS WAGON BY HORSE LOADED WITH HAY. OH! TO ENGAGE IN THAT KIND OF SERENITY NOWADAYS IS NEXT TO IMPOSSIBLE. I HEARD VOICES AND SAW IMAGES OF THIS CASTLE. MY BEAUTIFUL WIFE TAUGHT ME TO VISUALIZE THE CASTLE AND HEAR ALL THE VOICES. I HAVE HAD ANCESTORY FROM COUNTY CORK.

TIMBERS, MCCORMICKS, KELLYS WERE AMONG THE MANY ANCESTORS I MAY HAVE HAD (THERE COULD BE MORE) THE IMAGES I GOT WERE OF 2 TALL TOWERS, A FEW CHURCHES AND A DRAWBRIDGE THAT TOOK MY BREATH AWAY. IT WAS A MAJESTIC DRAWBRIDGE WITH THICK CHAINS TO HOLD THE MIGHTY DOOR WHICH SEALS THE CASTLE FROM THE WORLD. IN FRONT OF THE DRAWBRIDGE WAS A BEAUTIFUL TREE. IT GAVE OFF A SHADE THAT ONE CAN FALL ASLEEP UNDER. THE VOICE INSIDE KEPT CALLING TO ME AS I NEARED THE CASTLE. I AM GUESSING THAT THE FEMALE VOICE WAS FROM AN ANCESTOR LONG DEAD AND ONLY MY EARS WERE TUNED TO THE SOOTHING SOUND. I WOULD ALWAYS FIND MYSELF GOING BACK TO THAT CASTLE

IF ONLY IN MY MIND. I WAS STRUCK WITH ANOTHER VISION OF ME RUNNING TO THE CHURCH WITH A PIECE OF HOLY RELIC THAT BELONGS TO THE CHURCH. THE RELIC WAS A GOLD CROSS THAT BELONGED TO A PRIEST THAT HAD PASSED AWAY. HE WAS THE PRIEST OF THE CHURCH AND HAS GIVEN HIS LIFE TO THE LORD. THE CROSS WAS AS SHINY AS A NEW PENNY. IT GLISTENED IN THE SUNLIGHT; I WAS BLESSED BY GOD TO MOVE THIS TO ITS RIGHTFUL PLACE. THE VICAR'S NAME WAS (HOW FITTING) SAUL. I GAVE HIM THE RELIC FOR THE PASTORS PURPOSE WHOSE NAME WAS JOSEPH. HE WAS INSIDE THE CHURCH AWAITING MY SAFE ARRIVAL, SAYING THE RELIC (FROM WHAT I UNDERSTAND) THE HOLY ROSARY ARRIVED SAFELY. I HAVE HAD NO FURTHER VISIONS CONTAINING THIS UNIQUE BEAUTY AND SERENITY.

WHAT IS WRONG WITH OUR GOVERNMENT TODAY

BY BERNADINE MISURA

(4-30-07)

Okay let's play, what's wrong with our government today? Good question, where do I begin? For starters let me ask how did our government become such a zoo? It even smells more like a zoo, more than a real zoo does. The Earth God Created now smells of vile evil.

For instance when someone is running for a political position: they claim that they are for certain rights, no matter what they may be, but when they win and they are voted in; they change their minds and they claim they never said what they believe in or they say that's a lie! I say don't even try, but I do ask, why lie?

I got another question: how did they get the right to decide women's health decisions? Who gave them this right? Such as abortion, I bet whoever they were they now have regrets and they would like to get it changed after changing their minds, let's just keep in mind God knows and sees all, you will take a great fall.

Oh yeah for those of you who think because you want to change God's rules and laws just for fun you know you have no rights? Who gave the right to hurt the innocents of all of God's Creatures? How dare you? For what gay right, Ha! Go away, you have no rights, but you still enjoy your gay parade.

As for the people who are trying to separate Church and State, I don't know what you are thinking, you claim that our Forefathers made all the rules and laws; you are part correct they wrote them on paper. God wrote them on Tablets: first anybody remember Moses and the Ten Commandments, the One holding up the House of Representatives, did you even know why? Or are you too dumb to figure it out?

The biggest wrong done to our government is when they didn't stop the invasions of the Mexicans, and Haitians, these were and still are very bad mistakes and now we have the Arabs and China men who would like to make us an end, let's not forget about the Africans as well, this is too much of hell.

Life is going to rough for all of us because these so called people we vote in, are committing great sins and using us and Jesus as a clutch, ask yourself why do you allow it because you think they are perfect, only God, Mary, and Jesus, are Perfect, you think the politicians will work around the Laws of God for you? Why do you think you are that special, you have GOT to know in your little minds this just isn't true, what is wrong with you?

These are most of the reasons why our government is all but destroyed, when are all of you ever going to understand that The Almighty God is on his way to make all this vile evil go away! So you had better shape up and wake up before it's too late for you.

You want to know when this all really started: when the white man landed on Plymouth Rock and succeeded in taking all they need and all native lands, well, it's time for the natives to take back what is theirs and it's time for God and us to take our stand.

WHAT'S WRONG WITH YOU

BY BERNADINE MISURA
(10-17-06)

This is for all the people who like to bitch, moan, or complain, or those who get a thrill out of poking fun of someone even when you either don't know or understand their situation, I ask you what is wrong with you? Is it because people didn't treat you right when you were being beaten, this is not a good reason to make someone else feel sad or bad. How about the criminal why do you think you are tough and cool? You are not anything but ugly, and cruel, away with you.

This is for the people who are on a power trip, and to you everyone else is treated like they don't exist, you don't care who you hurt, you roll your eyes like you are annoyed, you just want your prize. Well I tell you where you will go if you don't start being a bit more charitable, until your cup over flows maybe then you can fill the void. What is wrong with you how dare you?

This question is for everyone who thinks it's cool to hurt one of God's innocents, the four legged critters and creatures, as for the ones who enjoy dirty sex and love to destroy the evidence, such as God's unborn children, these babies are not yours to take and kill with even just a pill those babies belong to the Good Lord, didn't you ever hear of thou Shalt not kill? What is really wrong with you?

This is for the sinners who want to destroy the work of God, so they can have religion their way on their time, I already know God and His Son Jesus will say to hells highway for you: those parents of soldiers who complain and about the choice their child took, what is wrong with you? To ridicule the road your child chose, shame on you, you do have more than blood on your nose. None of you will ever get to Heaven unless you change your ways: a good start would be confession, maybe many sessions with a Priest, a Vessel of God. What is wrong with all of you?

WHEN THE HOLY SPIRIT DESCENDS

BY BERNADINE ZIEGLER
(5-15-13)

When the Holy Spirit Descends into hell what happens to Him: does anyone care, do you say, oh well that is the End of Him. Others say only time will tell, I say to them how dare you not care. He gave His Life for you and you say let me be. I say you will never go anywhere or be anything.

Don't you understand God is giving up His Only Son to die for all of us and even you, and then He was sent to hell to fight off all of our original sins that we have caused? He Ascended into Heaven to save us all from our destruction.

You see He came down from Heaven to tell all of us that He is Here for us this you can trust, He also came down to tell us that He Loves us all that much, so why can't all of us Love Him as much, even if there is only Three? Why can't we all just give it a try if not I ask all of you why?

Didn't you all ever wonder why there are so many different religions split up from His Holy Church? Of these there are too many. It is because evil wants to take you away far away from His Love, and getting to go home with Him to the Promised Land Above.

So I ask again, why can't we just stand together as One Church, His Church. And say Lord I am here, I love you, I adore you and I do Thank You for everything You do for me, I am unworthy. Can we all just try, this I am sure He will hear you. What do you say let's send our love?

WHERE DID OHIO GO?

BY BERNADINE ZIEGLER
(7-13-10)

Where did Ohio go? I look out my window every day; I stand for a while just to contemplate over all the colors. I see the birds in the trees, the wind kissing the ground again and again just to say Hello my friend, how have you been? The grass is so green and the ground so fresh some of it rich and black some of it is brown. Oh how you turn His Earth upside down? Is this Ohio as I know it? Ah! No I don't think so! So where did it go?

Then as I watch my trees sway all day, the slow kissing breeze, trying to keep the cold at bay, I see everyone is in a hurry to go where but do I really care? Why can't they just see your awesome light turn on the day?

Why are there no children at play and getting skinned knees from the games in the autumn leaves? Children don't play anymore outdoors for the risk of being taken away from their family and friends. Why can't people just leave them alone then they can enjoy? Where are the bees, no honey in the trees? Why can't you just listen to the songs of the birds? I ask why does everybody want to harm someone or something. I ask you just stop and think? Where did Ohio really go? I may never know.

As I continue to look around: I make no sound, I shake my head instead and I ask the question to myself, where did Ohio go? Now when I go outside the only things I hear are cars going quickly by. Down all the streets who are they really going to meet? Why can't they just stop and see God's beautiful Nature show in its simplicity. This is not Ohio.

What has happened to stopping and lending a hand to people who are in distress? What happened to sharing, caring, and giving of charity? It just doesn't seem very clear to me. Oh God, how and why did Ohio get this way? How do I make this go away? God's World is such a mess. Now everyone says you're on your own, please leave me alone! I say just put down that computer or phone, forget the rest believe me that is best, you need to stop and breathe in some of nature's bounty and subside.

Go outside, slow down, sit down, you don't need to make a sound to listen for the tide it's a feeling you just can't describe just really listening to the trees sway so very slow, the breeze touches your nose, you can't help but smile.

Smell that air, the feeling you can't compare, the birds flying, the squirrel scurrying they are not in a hurry they have no worry. Enjoy the sun and have some of your own fun, the day is not done, no matter the season you really have no other reason to not enjoy God's wonderful Gift He gave to all of us to see. You just would rather destroy his land, why can't you understand? That your behavior is just wrong!

What happened to helping out God's Creatures, especially the four legged ones, watching them roam, forage and play all day and then stop to take a little rest, I take a big breath of air I can feel it all the way down to my breast, I feel this way even in the snow, I think to myself where do we really have to go? I smile just watching the animals enjoy natures delight, I ask myself why can't we all just do this maybe for just one day, you will never feel the same way.

So why is everyone so busy, always in a tizzy, forget your plight and go outside for the night just look up and see God's beautiful Lights, why is everyone more interested in stripping and throwing God out of their lives and out the door? Instead of seeing His Eternal Light shine in the sky at night, does it really give you such a fright? Don't you see God Loves us and gives us so much?

This is not Ohio, not the one I remember, go out in your yard, get out of your car, KNEEL on the ground don't make a sound put your ear down and listen what do you hear? That is God's Gift the trees, air, water, creatures, critters, we all come from God's Hand, without Him: the world will surely go away, never to brighten the way or light the day and shine in the night. So I ask again: this time out loud where did Ohio go? Where did Ohio really go? Please I beg of you, just let me know.

WHY CONFESSION?

BY BERNADINE ZIEGLER
(12/12/14)

Why confession, when your parents tell you when you are young you must go to confession just like an order or else suffer they even call you an atheist or pagan, then you ask why? Why must I go to confession, what do I have to confess I am a kid, how do I get out of it? Don't you really ask yourself why am I so afraid to go see a priest what have I really done wrong, but you really think what right does a priest have to give me absolution or the right to speak for God, and Jesus, no answer.

Your parents come back by saying you must get clean. You think to yourself from what have I done wrong? I don't understand! These words you want to shout out, but you know you get a smack in the mouth so you think how am I going to figure this out, do my parents even know, why don't they answer me why don't they tell me help me understand. Oh! My frustration but you do as your parents ask.

The whole time you are waiting your turn, you do your best to find a way out what do I say what do I confess to? You are next in line what am I going to do? You feel burning from inside, you can't breathe but all you can think about how do I leave. The door opens the sinner leaves the light turns green for you to go, all you want to do is cry to the point that you would rather die than you go inside the room you call gloom, sometimes to you it feels like a tomb.

Everyone is waiting for you to go, everyone is watching you what do you do? Then you finally make your choice you finally find your voice and say to the priest bless me father for I have sinned but you are still thinking from what or how have I sinned somehow you find the right words from within your heart, you are still really nervous, for some reason it still feels like a death sentence.

Then when you are all done believe me you will not think that was fun not at all, but you will think to yourself that wasn't so bad that wasn't hard I still don't understand but for some reason you feel different you feel better like a weight is off your shoulder you feel clean how can this be? You look at the cross at the man you say Lord I still don't understand why do I feel this way?

As you grow in life you still go to confession but you still don't know why, you still don't understand, you have a new thought do I really need to go, am I really getting everything I need why must I be clean when I just want to be free to be me, I don't understand why? Oh! My frustration. You can't help wondering what is this all really about, who is this all about?

You look up at the cross close your eyes think to him please Lord help me understand please Lord take my hand, just when you are about to leave the church He comes to you and says come here child take my hand I will help you understand. He takes your hand He says I love you my daughter do you love me? This question makes you want to drop to your knees but do you know why? No! Then you finally say yes! Lord I do.

Now that I am all grown up I don't have any more frustration, I must admit it did take me a while to understand but he was always there to help me and to take my hand. I always go to confession why you ask? No matter what my situation no matter why I feel pain and sorrow, I always feel so much better I am happier because I love Him, The Great I Am, and evil can never make its penetration, this is why I am always at peace. Please don't be afraid of him

So I say to you no matter what you have done or have failed to do in life, The Lord forgives everyone, all you have to say is Lord forgive me! He loves all. Please come with me to see the Great I Am, you will be at peace just like me, He and I will help you understand help you have and know His love for you. So I ask again will you come with me my friend, I ask you can you, do you believe me do you believe in Him? All you have to do is love Him.

My Pastor asked me to help others understand the joys of confession help them know what they should be getting out of it. The peace, joy, and the tranquility of His love, this I must admit scared me a little. Does he know what he is really asking of me or don't I really understand what he is asking of me? For some time I just wasn't sure how to do this? I pray I never let him down, I pray this is what he meant but his words I did never forget.

CHEROKEE PRAYER

WRITTEN BY MARK ZIEGLER
ON 7/6/06

God in Heaven above please protect the one we love
We honor all You Created. As we pledge our hearts,
Lives together.

We honor Mother Earth, and ask for
Our marriage to be abundant, and grow stronger thru
The seasons, we honor fire- and ask that our union be
Warm and glowing with love in our hearts.

We honor wind-as we sail thru life safe and calm,
As in our fathers arms.

We honor water-to clean and soothe
Our marriage- that it may never thirst for love.

All the forces of the universe you created, we pray
For harmony and true happiness, and we forever
Will grow young together Amen!

DEAR FORGOTTEN ONE

WRITTEN BY BERNADINE ZIEGLER
ON 3-12- 11

Dear Forgotten One, even though we haven't met I am still writing you a letter, to tell you, you're not alone in this world where ever you may roam, I know you have no home, no I don't know your name whether creature, critter. God and I love you just the same even if you are small as a mouse or as large as a house, or even a plain John or Jane. You will know this just by his kiss.

I happen to know this because I was almost you, then I found out that he loves me too, you probably think you are going to hell only time will tell. Please remember this it's never to late for you just pray all day and say God, Jesus lord help me, help me take my troubles away that is what I do and that is why I say this to you, believe me it's true.

Dear Forgotten One, I know you don't know what to say or do but I'll still pray for you, I also know you want to scream and cry out loud but you're afraid to make a sound, I know so did I. I also just wanted to die so I say dry your eyes and come to see Jesus with me to his church, believe me you will feel so much love and peace with him you will be happily surprised, you will realize you have never been alone.

GOD IS CALLING

BY BERNADINE ZIEGLER
(5-1-13)

Ring, ring, aren't you going to answer that? God is calling you, you ask why me? What do I do, what does He want from me? God calls all of us, to do his work to spread his word the good news, such as Abram, or Moses and the Ten Commandments, do you remember the Ten Commandments? The one and only laws written by God and given to Moses for us to follow, and obey. He loves us this much.

The (First) one is: I, The Lord, am your God; you shall not have other gods besides me, what does this mean? It's quite simple, you are to love God, the only god, the perfect God of all, and to obey him, and to believe in no others. It's just that simple. Under The Seven Deadly Sins, this falls under Greed. You wrong God you can never be free.

The (Second) one is: you shall not take the name of the Lord your God in Vain. What does this mean? I hear a lot of people committing this, they say his name to curse or use his name in a mean over tone in their speech, then they expect that He will do something for them, well, I tell you it doesn't work that way and will never work this way. Out of the Seven Deadly Sins, this falls under two of them: Envy and Vanity, this is not good!

The (Third) one is: remember to keep holy the Sabbath, what does this mean? To give the seventh day of the week just to the Lord God and nothing else. No shopping, no bill talk just God in his beautiful home; it is our job and right to love and serve the Lord. Why doesn't everyone do this? Why can't they just stop and say it's the Lord's Day. This falls under Sloth, why because we are all a little slow in loving the lord and his church.

The (Fourth) one is: honor thy father and mother, this just doesn't mean listen to what your father and mother tells you. It also means to obey what they tell you they love you and try to protect you. It also means to listen to and obey the Holy Mother Mary, and The Holy Father of all, it is his right to have the same love and respect. This one also falls under Sloth, because we are also slow in understanding not just our father and mother, but our Holy Mother Mary, and The Holy Father.

The (Fifth) one is: a hard one a lot of people have, they just don't get it. You shall not kill, then why is everyone aborting their babies? What gives you the right? What about all the stabbings, shootings, and just plain hurting creatures and God's critters, what gives any of you the right to disobey this law of God's? This one is really bad people, this one falls under four out of seven of the Deadly Sins, and I know you say oh! Really what ones? How about Anger, Envy, Greed, and Pride, to commit this awful crime you would have to have all of these sins in your heart.

The (Sixth) Commandment is: you shall not commit adultery, I can't tell you how many times this has been disobeyed, first thing is there is only one marriage, under God, there is no divorces permitted, no re-marrying. This falls under Lust, to commit this crime against God it would have to be Lust.

There is so much of this, how about sex out of wedlock, kids having sex and kids having kids. I can't tell you how much this goes on it just does. What gives any of you the right to commit these crimes against God, and you think you are not doing any wrong, well I tell you now you are doing wrong by God, I just ask you how, why must you let this go on?

The (Seventh) One is: you shall not steal, then why is that still going on today and people are just getting a slap on the wrist? You have no right to do any of this, I don't care about the why, I just want you to stop it! This is quite simply Greed, and that is all he wrote.

The (Eighth) Commandment is: you shall not bear false witness against your neighbor, what does this mean? Well it means that people have been telling others lies about a neighbor, just to upset their day, or destroy their lives, I ask why must you be so cruel? You have no right to do this to another. This one is pure Vanity, because you are so vain you want to hurt others, and in flick pain.

The (Ninth) One is: you shall not covet your neighbor's wife, what does this mean? no sex or other marriages after your spouse has passed on, God created man and then he created a woman for every man, you have no right to touch anyone that you didn't marry the first and only time given to you by God.

This one falls under two of the sins Lust and Pride, why because you're proud to take someone's love and you desire to do this.

The (Tenth) Commandment is: you shall not covet anything that belongs to your neighbor, this is just not the final commandment, and it says it all. You have no right to take anything that doesn't belong to you. The only thing you have a right to take or receive is God's love for you. This one falls under three of the sins, Envy, Pride, Greed, just think about it.

God will we ever understand that the Seven Deadly Sins, are connected to the Ten Commandments, because to go against the Commandments you must be committing the Deadly Sins. We must stop this and learn to love Christ instead.

If you and I do not follow these laws given to us from God out of love for us, then we have no right to receive the many blessings he will give to us such as His Eight Beatitudes, but there are many more in store when you give to him love and. devotion, Wow! What a notion, it is just this easy.

What are God's Beatitudes, well as best that I can guess is that they are: How blest are the poor in spirit the reign of God is theirs, (Two) is Blest too are the sorrowing; they shall be consoled, (Three) is Blest are the Lowly; they shall inherit the land, (Four) Blest are they who hunger and thirst for holiness; they shall have their fill, this one I really think we all are and that we should all continue to be they teach us humility.

The (fifth) Beatitude is Blest are they who show mercy; mercy shall be theirs, the (Sixth) is Blest are the single hearted; they shall see God, the (Seventh) Blest too the peacemakers; they shall be called Sons of God, and the (Eighth) Blest are those persecuted for holiness' Sake; the reign of God is theirs.

Don't you think we should strive for these gifts of God? Can't you imagine how special we all are to God? Why can't you understand it's just not these gifts we would receive from God there are others such as His Everlasting Love, His Grace, Hope, Guidance, Compassion, His Comfort. How could anyone not want these blessings?

How about His Holy Sacraments, the Lord wants us to follow these Sacraments to help understand the love and spirit of The Risen Christ, how could anyone not want this? How about Devine Mercy, the Sacraments, are given to us by God to help us get into Heaven, are you all really sure you don't want this?

You ask what are His Holy Sacraments, How do we follow them? There are seven of them and the (First) one is Baptism, when we are babies we are cleansed with Holy Water by a priest so we can be saved from our original sin and be children of God at the same time.

The (Second) one is Confirmation; this deepens our union with Christ and helps us proclaim our faith in Him before all others. The (Third) one is the Holy Eucharist; this is the body and blood of our Blessed Lord, and our spiritual food to nourish our union with Him. The (Fourth) is Penance, this restores our union with the lord because of disruption due to our sins, after most people accomplish these four Sacraments they just plain stop there, Why? Why do you stop?

When the last three are just as important to accomplish for God as the other first four, the (Fifth) is Anointing of the sick, this helps us strengthen our union with Christ during those times of serious illness, I just think this could and should also mean a sickness in mind and soul that stopped us from loving the lord.

The (Sixth) is Holy Orders, this gives men the power of uniting or re-uniting believers with God through his Holy Vessels, now I know we all can't do this one but we can pray for these men who are wanting and now working for Christ. Then the last and final one, the (Seventh) Holy Matrimony, doesn't just mean it makes a man and a woman husband and wife, you must also be virgins of Christ, this gives you the right to live with God, for God and each other in His Grace.

Ring, ring, God is calling, can't you hear it? It's for you, When are you going to answer His call, or would you rather take a great fall? That is all.

MY GUIDING LIGHT,
MY SHINING STAR.

WRITTEN BY BERNADINE ZIEGLER
ON 1-28-11

Jesus Christ, you will always be my guiding light, my shining star,
In my heart, I pray we may never part, in my body may your Holy Light,
Burn forever bright, in my soul, let your love flow. Please soothe me,
Don't let me go.

Lord Jesus, I know you hear me, see me, and love me, for this I know
Lord , it's no secret I need you this is true, do you need me? Please
Guide me, to your loving arms. Please protect me.

You and Mother Mary, are so perfect beyond compare I do not dare,
Even with my many faults, please love me, and with my many sins,
Please forgive me. When you call upon me, I answer yes! Lord, it is me
I think to myself how could this be? What is It you need of me?
All I want to do in life is to please thee. Please heal me.

God, I will always ask of you be my Guiding Light, my Shining Star.
Hear me, come to me, save me, bless me, and to thank you for everything
You do for me. I love you.

HIS HOLY HAND

BY BERNADINE ZIEGLER
(2-18-13)

Oh God, please take my hand and teach me how to get them to understand by your grace, guide me to hear and obey your holy truth, in your beautiful home where I would rather be, being in your church I always feel at peace. Because of your chosen priests, believing and loving you I really can't think of anything better to do can you?

By your grace I pray for mercy and to have pity on me, please lord with your Holy Hand help me stand on my own two feet, so I can tell all these sinners, that being in your Blessed Arms, there is no better place, and maybe someday with His Holy Hand he will touch yours and my face.

Oh how do I get you all to understand that God is love and if you don't extend your hand and say here I am lord, what about me? Please love me too, by taking my hand help me stand, I pray for mercy and pity, I give you my obedience, from you he will never stray.

Then he'll extend His Holy Hand and say come with me, I'll pick you up even if you can't stand on your own two feet, his love, guidance, and grace, and seeing His Holy Face, All I would be able to say is why me, Lord I'm such a disgrace?

This is why I always pray every day so he won't wipe me away, with just one swipe of His Holy Hand, our world would never be again. So we all need to come together as one and accept and learn His Holy Word, so we can share in His Love with a big hug with the lord above, I think this sounds great, do you? I know I can't wait to be held in God's Arms, I tell you true.

HIS HOLY STONE

BY BERNADINE ZIEGLER
(1/19/15)

Did you ever hear that expression don't leave any stone unturned? Well I can honestly say I didn't know what that meant until the Lord put this Poem in my head, so what is His Holy Stone? Where is it, what ever happened to it, what does it look like? Well I guess that will always be a great mystery, but I do know it covered the place where he rose from the dead.

From what I understand it is very heavy and very hard to move. I also heard that it is a large round stone. One that covered the opening of the His Burial Home, I heard it had some etchings on it. The etchings are the shapes of the animals and insects around His World that He chose as blessed , they consisted of sea, land, and sky animals of all kinds, but I don't know how many in all.

The animal's pictures went into a circle all around the stone and I know there is one in the middle as big as light above all the rest as if to reach for the sky can anyone guess what animal it is? It is His White Dove, and a cross above its head and a heart displayed on the doves chest to symbolize His Love.

Why isn't anyone speaking of this Holy Relic? It is mentioned in the Holy Bible. Has everyone forgotten about Jesus' tomb? SHAME ON ALL OF YOU!!! Jesus DIED for ALL of you. Makes you think, huh?

I just have a question or two for all of you; didn't you ever wonder what happened to His Holy Stone, where did it go? Is it broken or is it all in one piece still I guess no one will ever tell? I know the answer to who moved the stone to let Jesus out but do any of you really know the answer? Why isn't anyone telling of the size and weight of the stone or its location oh! The frustration but if you got to see it oh! The jubilation why doesn't anyone really wonder?

HOW TO SAY I'M SORRY TO A TREE

BY BERNADINE ZIEGLER
(1-27-13)

Every time I look outside at my front and side yard, there was the five of you, two were very sick, and the other three trees were on their way, when I go outside to see and feel your trunks, all I can feel is your pain and hear you saying it's okay! Please take my pain away! I said no! I won't! The trees said you have too, I replied, "you make shade for me"; they said it's got to be.

I know this is silly of me to cry for five trees, I said no! I don't want to let you go! I thought to myself what has come over me, I know they are trees but they're beautiful because they are God's trees, I felt the tree trunk again, the tree said, "please don't disgrace me by making me fall"! All the five trees agreed please let us go! I finally said okay with tears running down my face, I'll cut you all down, so you feel no more pain, but it won't stop my rain.

Now I look outside I can't help to think, what if I left them there maybe just for one more year so I could look at their beauty and watch the birds sing and play in the trees every day. I know they are gone but not forgotten it was very hard to say good-bye to my trees, it's like they are and always will be a part of me. Now that they are gone, I know there will be more sunny days. Everyone should love and thank a tree for the things they give such as clean air and for their simple beauty.

How does one say good-bye to a tree? You put your hand on the trunk of the tree and say tree hear me please! I have to let you go, and want to let you know I must cut you down so you don't take a fall, you have served me well, I'm very sorry for what I must do, but I can't save any of you, I'll miss you and never will forget you, but I didn't know what else to do, please forgive me. This is how everyone should say good-bye to a tree.

I HAVE SEEN, I HAVE HEARD

BY BERNADINE ZIEGLER
(1/7/15)

I have seen, I have heard so many things some good and some very bad, the bad things I don't wish to speak about. All you have to do is look around to figure it out. The good things I have seen and heard are the things I wish to write this poem about. What are these good things you ask? Well, start with the Lord God; after all if we don't start with Him would we have anything good or bad? Please Lord don't go away! I will never stray!

I ask all of you have you seen Him have you heard what He has to say? I don't just mean by seeing Him on the cross. I have seen Him in many visions, all uniquely wonderful, until you have opened your eyes, you will never see and feel the beauty of this, and until you open your ears and heart to Him you will never know His Many Wonders He has planned for us. I don't know why I have been given this honor to Know and Love Him, I will forever treasure these days, all I can say is Lord bless all my days.

Have you ever heard the hymn in church "Eyes have not seen ears have not heard" what God has ready for those who love Him the spirit of Love. Come give us the mind of Jesus. The next time you sing or hear it, really listen and feel the words they are all true, when you feel these words a feeling of warmth will come over you this feeling is Jesus, coming to you this is the Lord calling to you, as he has done for me, because He loves you too.

KEYS

BY BERNADINE ZIEGLER
(12/13/14)

My husband gave me another challenge, he asked me to write a poem about keys, I thought for just a few minutes. Keys, why keys? Then it came to me, what is really so good about keys? What do they do, what are they really good for? Well let's think this out. I know they come in many shapes and sizes but what else are they good for?

Well I know they need to hang on a ring and I'm sure that they are also used to open things, don't get me wrong but I think keys can even turn on a car. This is all true, I stop and think again what else can keys be used for besides opening up a window or door, can keys be used for decoration, maybe oh! How about keys for a baby? Such as a toy for a girl or boy!

You know there is another kind of key that isn't made of metal or plastic, how about when someone tells a riddle in order to figure out the answer you have to decipher a solution to the riddle and that would also be a key as in key solution to a problem, then I stop and think isn't there another kind of key? Did you hear that expression that God has the keys to Heaven and hell and that someday He was going to toss them away?

When I think about this, I think that is crazy why would He do that? When the Lord God is the REAL key to Heaven and hell. Because after all He is the Creator isn't He? He is not going to toss himself away, but we do! Did you ever hear another expression you can earn a key to Heaven or hell! How can this be, don't you think this thought is really crazy and completely out of the question? Why would anyone want to throw Him out? Furthermore, why would anyone in his or her right mind want to earn a key to hell?

So you see there are so many different kind of keys, there is a key for all kinds of situations, life is a puzzle, which key do I want? Oh! My frustration, Oh! I can't decide! What is wrong with me? I choose God and all keys to get to Heaven, at least purgatory that is the last of this story. O, come on people, let's GET REAL with ourselves, There's only one way to get a key to Heaven, that is to LOVE GOD totally and completely. It seems as though we are always telling God our plans, he will chuckle and tell us His.

MARRIAGE OR THE CHURCH
WHAT IS THE DIFFERENCE

BY BERNADINE ZIEGLER

(1/25/15)

When I first thought of this poem I really had to think it out. Is there really a difference between the two? My husband said this is going to be a hard subject for you. I thought to myself can this really be this hard, is this why everybody is doing so much wrong, are we really all this confused? If so, we all lose! What then are we supposed to do? How are we supposed to fix this, how did things get so out of hand? This is a very good question. For a few folks it is a complicated decision but don't you ask yourself why, why did I really make this bad decision? Why is this so hard to understand God's plan? How do I get all of you to understand?

The best way I can go about this, is do all of you remember the Holy Sacraments I do believe there are seven in all, I know you are saying what does that have to do with it? Well, I say everybody should think about the Seven Holy Sacraments they are given to us from Jesus, right at our birth such as our baptism, to take away original sin, but this is just the first one but most people stop here some but very few go on to the second one the Confirmation, this deepens our union with Christ, and helps us proclaim our faith in Him before others, but then why do people stop at this one? Why do you tell God this lie?

Why do they do this, some but very few actually do take the Holy Eucharist, after this do you really think it's over and that you are done? Well, I have news for you this just isn't true, God loves you but you must follow through there are at least three more that you must do in the order that Jesus has laid the laws out for you, such as Penance,

Anointing, the last one is up to you Holy Orders Or Matrimony. A lot of people skip some and go right to marriage but is it really the right thing to do surely your marriage won't be a delight because you do not have God's burning light, so I ask why don't you all do right by God?

I am sure you all still don't understand but I will come at it another way because you all are under the impression that any marriage has God's Okay, well I have to tell you that is not true because one you must have purity, virginity, obedience to do God's Will in Holy Matrimony to do this you must acquire all the Holy Sacraments, My husband and I acquired all of these and I couldn't imagine it any other way, I don't even want to try. But I can take heart in knowing when we die my husband and I will at least get to purgatory on the way to Heaven. How could no one want this?

But the original question marriage or the church, what is the difference? Still needs an answer and the answer is there is no real difference between marriage or the church, why? you ask well, let's think of it this way a priest has to also follow the Holy Sacraments as well as we do but the stop at Holy Order because if you think about it they are married also the difference they are married to the church for us to save us from evil hell, and we marry a spouse of our choice but we still have to have the wedding in the church so by God's Grace we will become one with His Voice and be able to see His Face.

But if you still are not understanding the truth about all of this well I'll give you another situation, one day I e-mailed my priest, keep in mind this is a Holy Man but his answer to me is you can't always get what you want and he called me and all wives being needy and the one that takes everything in the marriage he accused me of being demanding and not giving I must admit I took great offense to this. Don't get me wrong I love this man but he has no right to make such a comparison, when he can never understand.

I was very angry which you should never do to a priest but begged God for advice and He said His priest was wrong and to teach His priest the truth, so I wrote him a very strong e-mail but before I finished I showed my husband what he said and he also got very angry and to my surprise he also wrote him some very strong words, we both double teamed him, I still ask God to forgive me for this but He says His priest needed to know the truth because he could never understand our situation because it can never be his.

So the answer to the question marriage or the church what is the difference well, marriage is the church so there is no difference. My husband and I chose marriage and our priest chose the church but we are the same because we are all part of the church we must live for the church, we must follow and obey.

And stand as one in The Holy Church and Jesus Lord God's laws set for the church. So you see we are not here for us, we are here to do His Will by this way alone. It is the only way we will ever get to see Thee in His Holy Home called Heaven.

MY GUARDIAN

WRITTEN BY BERNADINE MISURA
ON 8-20-06

I was having a lot of depression problems, such as nervous break downs and emotional pain from family, I tried to end my life for so many different reasons, and at least four different ways, I only had one friend that I was aware of, keep in mind that is a classic symptom, then I heard a voice shout don't you dare finish what you are doing, if you do then I can not help you anymore.

I couldn't see anyone that could have belonged to this voice it was so forceful and it sounded and felt very powerful, but for some reason I do not know why I wasn't even asking the voice 'who are you'? With the power of the voice, I did not dare, the voice went on to say I need you for something else, for what he didn't tell me and I wasn't about to ask.

I have never been so afraid in my life, I asked out loud
'Lord have you been my guardian this whole time'?

I thought to myself, wait! This can't be the lord, I said out loud 'Are you the lord they called The Most High? No answer! All I could think of is why me, I said again, 'Lord is it you, are you still there'? He answered and said 'I am He, I am here'.

I was in a quiet shock while thinking ,'why me Lord,' I might of even said it out loud. He said again,' I can't save you if you still want to die, If you finish, you will surely go straight to hell.' He said no more, I said,' Lord , 'you have been my guardian, why didn't you tell me?

I didn't know anyone was there, I didn't know anyone really cared, Lord, if you will stay by my side, I will stop trying to end it all. I plead for mercy, Lord, why me? Lord, have pity on me, I beg you please.

He replied, 'If you decide you want to live, I will always be by your side. I said, Lord I will try, I don't want to die, but it's going to be hard, I will need you all the time, I beg you please forgive me, I love thee, I need you to always be my guardian.

MY LITTLE POUCH OF HOPE

BY BERNADINE ZIEGLER
(12-17-12)

My little pouch isn't very big just the right size to fit in my pocket, I carry it with me all the time. It's made with buffalo and maybe deer skins, and a little black string. It contains items of no real value to anybody else but me. So you ask why I carry it with me.

Native American squaws used to always carry little pouches with them I never knew what was in them, I guess maybe spices for the cooking, but mine does not, my little pouch is very special to me, because the things it carries are from God, these items are even blessed by him.

How do I arrive at that conclusion you ask? I pray to the Lord Jesus and God a lot sometimes I think for some reason they didn't hear me or they are tired of hearing from me, just when I start thinking that way, they leave me a token or some kind of message, gift, to tell me that they heard me.

I can't help but smile when I find these gifts just about where I am standing or praying to them, then just after I tell them thank you for the gift and lending an ear, I place the item in my little green brown pouch, and that is how it also became my pouch of courage, protection, and hope, it also reminds me that God and Jesus are always with me.

MY WISHING HOUSE

BY BERNADINE MISURA
(10-3-06)

My wishing house, oh how sometimes I wish I was a church mouse,
So I can be with the Lord, day and night, Oh how that would be such a
Delight, I could be alone in his beautiful home forever to roam, as long
As I was quiet, I could just be with my thoughts and the good Lord, he
Always helped me work things out.

My wishing house is always so beautiful with the stained glass windows
To the burning flames of His Candles, I can't help but look at His Feet
on the Cross and wonder, I feel the pain, oh how evil has left such a
stain, My wishing house can be found anywhere, all around the world.

What place could be better than being in the house of the Lord, he will
Keep you warm he will soothe your soul; he will even give you a loving
Hug when no one else will. He is always waiting to console you, no
matter What you may do. If for some reason you don't care to understand
what he Does for you, then I got three words for you shame on you!

ONE'S BROKEN CROSS

BY BERNADINE ZIEGLER
(12/14/14)

When you see one's broken cross what is the first thing you think what is the first thing you want to say you still are looking at it what is it you keep seeing then you finally say to your friend oh! That was a pretty cross now what are you going to do with it? You ask your friend what would you do with it would you just toss it away or say that is okay or would you mourn the loss, why would one feel this way or would you have any feeling at all?

Then your friend asks can you fix it and if so would it be the same would it look good again you continue looking at the broken cross and ask in your thoughts, what do I do with you? You finally think why do I feel this way, it feels like it is calling to you help me please help me, you hear it again help me. You pick it up put the broken pieces in your hand you hold it like a baby but you just want to cry you feel like something is torn from you. Than you finally answer your friend with a tear in your eye and say yes! Fixing it I will give a try.

There is another form of a broken cross this you may never understand and that is when Christ says pick up your cross and walk with me, I know at first you think why me, what does that mean? When you figure this out what do you do what do you say? Most people would not say a thing, moments go by you finally say no! I can't do that I wouldn't even try. This is how your cross became broken and you become forsaken your bonds with God and Christ are forever gone you know allowing this is so very wrong.

You take some more time and pray at His Cross, the thought comes to you a feeling comes over you, is my cross with Him broken? How does one fix this broken cross? The feeling of this broken cross is too horrible to mention but I guess it would feel like losing a great friend, one that was always there. How does one fix this broken cross, good question but the answer is very easy.

All you have to do is look at Him on the cross pray to Him say Lord I'm sorry please pity me, I ask for mercy help me, and also say thank you, may I still walk with you Lord? He will always smile and say come child be with me. So you see your cross has become repaired, this can be always achieved when you believe so never deceive, remember He will always see. He said once more pick up your cross and walk with me.

THE BLANKET OF CHRIST

BY BERNADINE ZIEGLER
(4-2-13)

I have heard of the Blood of Christ, which was out poured for us, I have heard of the Body of Christ, which was given to us to eat. I have even heard of the Shroud of Turin, It was His Body Wrappings made of linen, the Tomb of Christ, where He rose from the dead, I have even heard of the Crown of Christ, the Crown of Thorns He wore on His Blessed Head when He was Crucified, but you ask what is the Blanket of Christ?

What does The Blanket of Christ feel like, what is it made of? This is a very good question; it is made of His Love for all of us. Is it soft and warm? Yes! It is very soft and warm, Oh! I pray someday you will know the feeling of being wrapped up in His Love, being held and carried in His Loving Arms, Oh! And to feel His Soft Warm Embrace and the smile on His Loving Face for all of us, I pray we will know all of this one day.

Don't you see it, it is just as important and special to me and it should also be to you, just like the Birth of Christ, Christmas, the Tomb of Jesus, and His Resurrection, I know you ask how's that, what does the Blanket look like? Again all good questions: Well, I'll tell you to the best of my recollection. (Pause) (Kneel) on the word Resurrection.

Well, all I really know is when I have prayed to the Lord by saying, Lord help me, save me, pick me up when I fall, Lord warm me, I am so cold even my inner soul, please Lord help me. Just when you are about to give up because you think He didn't hear you and all you can do is cry and ask yourself, why? Why did I even try? Then you say Lord forgive me, just when you are at pure exhaustion.

He comes to you and simply says I heard you my child, He picks you up not just with His Hands but with His Forgiveness and Guidance, He wraps you up not just in His Arms but with his Love and Comfort, He doesn't just warm you up with a white blanket, He does it with His gentle touch, He loves us all so much, he even heals your inner soul with just a simple smile, Oh, how it glows for miles. As he is carrying you He says come with me, for you are safe with me.

Just like in my favorite poem called Foot Prints, how He picks up the sinner and carried him to safety, from evil, despair, and all his suffering of going nowhere, this is what the Lord also did for me, just remember this, when you are wrapped up in the Lord you are always going somewhere, you will have Everlasting Love, have I ever seen his White Dove?

Oh! How I love being wrapped in the Blanket of Christ, His Smile is just so bright, it lights up the night, and being held in His loving Arms is so comforting to me, it's beyond compare, to hear His Voice say, you're safe with Me, I'll take care of you! It soothes my inner soul, I am finally at peace, there is no more suffering, and this is known as the Blanket of Christ.

THE BLESSED TRINITY

BY BERNADINE ZIEGLER

(2-15-13)

What is the Blessed Trinity, you ask? Well it says in the Holy Bible, or some people call it the Good Book, if you take a look it will say the Holy Trinity, is Three in One. The Father, Son, and the Holy Ghost; who I adore the most.

You ask how they can be Three in One: I say God is The Father, Jesus, is His Son, and when Jesus Died on the Cross for us, His Spirit became the Holy Ghost, which is why I love Him the most because without Him, I wouldn't get to speak with God, or be saved by His Heavenly Host.

This is why we all should get down on one knee and pray to all Three, and say God, and your Blessed Divinity, I pray to you for pity and mercy, because if we don't then where would we all be? What would we really have? The answer is nothing! We would have nothing! We would also be nothing!

Just like the riddle my father told me, what is more powerful than God? What is more evil than the devil? The rich people want it, the poor people have it. Again the answer is nothing! For this I say Pray, Love and Obey the Blessed Trinity, Made of Three in One so we all don't become undone.

WHAT IS A PRIEST?

BY BERNADINE ZIEGLER
(12-14-10)

What is a priest? What makes a priest? I have asked myself these questions for years, with no avail, the best conclusion, as far as I can tell. What is a priest? He is a man some people just don't or refuse to understand but he still lends his hand, to help his fellow man, stand in faith, no matter if we think it's too late. He knows no cares, this is a priest. Alleluia, Amen.

What makes a priest? He is not just one of God's chosen by His Holy Hand, he is a simple man who loves and teaches the Scriptures, The Lord's Gospels just like Jesus, with his Apostles, but does any of the church parishioners really care? Do they just stop in and stare? At least they are there. Does anyone ask him hey! How was your day? Or are you feeling okay? Do we even ask these priests, are you tired? How or did you get any sleep, I pray it is always deep.

What makes a priest? Knowing he will always be there in times of trouble or despair, no matter the time, day or night, whether there is snow, ice, rain, or sun, or moon light, somehow he is always there for our care no matter his day, Does he show any pain, or strain, no! Somehow he always remains strong, just tending to the Sheppard's Flock, he bares no worries for his own home or where he may roam, even when he is maybe in a hurry, and he just carries merrily, on and on.

What is a priest? This man is always there to comfort us from our fears, failures, cares and woes with this man as your priest; he is a blessing to say the least. He will be there to help us through, to help us pick up our cross, and deal with our own situations, no matter his or our station, no matter his or God's strife in life.

A priest gives up everything to save our mortal souls, from evils reign, and to cleanse us from our sins from within, he has one goal in his life to help us prepare for His Holy Light, when it's our time to say good night, for the rest of our earth life. This man will always share with us a prayer, to ease us out of despair, he will always care. He may not know us but he and God, will always love, and be devoted, to us this you can trust.

This man works hard for The Great I Am, please take a moment and say God bless you, may the Lord keep and guide you and thank you, by giving him a hug, a tap on the shoulder, or take and shake his hand. Maybe someday we will all understand the trials and tribulations of this man. Alleluia, Amen.

What is a priest, from the Pope on down to his weary monk, they all have one job in common, and that is to bring us all back around to His Church, to love and not just understand His Holy Word, but to obey, and to bid hail to His Holy Crown. Alleluia and Amen.

His church started out as one, now it has become undone some of His Holy Sheep has fallen or gone to sleep, we need to learn how to forgive and pray, and to have pity on them, but we also need to pray mercy for all of us, Please don't make a fuss, we need to become one church, again to put up a good fight against the evil from within all of us, yes! God gave us choice, but we need to have one voice for him, to get to see and be with his angels, and witness heaven's delight when we are called to make that flight. Alleluia, Amen.

WHAT IT TAKES TO MAKE A PRIEST

༺ ༻

WRITTEN BY BERNADINE ZIEGLER
ON 3-7-13

You know I took confirmation class to understand my Catholicism, during the class my teacher Father Schleicher, was asking me all the questions, because he knew somehow, I was getting all the answers from Jesus, then one day he asked me are you sure you're not a priest? I didn't know what to say, about a second went by, I smiled at him, I said no! Father I don't think I'm a man, but you can check!

You can imagine the shock in the room, mine as well, the Father did a laugh cough and said no! That won't be necessary, all I could think is thank God, One day he thought he should apologize, I said no Father no apology is necessary, I said I'm glad I could help.

Father Schleicher, has sadly passed away, a day doesn't go by without me thinking of my teacher, God's Holy Vessel. No one will ever replace him.

Don't get me wrong there's nothing bad about being a man, I have even thought about what my life would be like if I was a man, if I was a man, the first thing I would do is become a priest, the first requirement, is being a man. I do love God and I would give my life back to him as he did for us, to cleanse us of our sins, I can't think of a better job than to be a Vessel of God, but alas I'm not a man.

How do I get you to understand? What it really takes to be a priest, such as the First Priest, Jesus Christ, King of Peace, he started it all by giving his life for us, going into hell then ascending into heaven and giving Saint Peter the keys, to His Church our church today, by saying those famous words upon thy rock you will build My Church! And that is what he did he built the first and only Church the Basilica, there can be no other.

So who is our first priest? His name is Love, when you love and want to serve the Lord you open a door to a world of so much more, by giving of yourself, and to serve others, to be completely devoted to do God's Will this would make you a priest, this is the first need of a priest this and humility, the ability to teach humility, to all humanity, this would make you a priest, to say the least.

WHERE DID THE BUFFALO GO?

BY BERNADINE MISURA

(2-17-07)

Where did the buffalo roam? Why are they not here? Where did all the buffalo go? Who took them all away? Who gave the white man the right to kill any of their lives? They are not God! I guess the only way to know is to get down on my knees and pray out loud to the Lord God and say lord where did all my buffalo go?

Yes! I am a Native American but unfortunately I did not get to see a buffalo, but I saw a few pictures of them in nature's simple beauty and that is why I am so angry with the white man who wanted nothing more than to destroy the race they call the American Indian, and take our land.

They will never understand it's not the American Indian they are hurting or destroying it's one of God's innocent creatures known as the mighty buffalo, all I know is they were wild and free and the white man had no right to harm or take any one's life that is only God's right to decide.

To this day the Native American are denied the fact that we are still slaves just like the mighty buffalo forever never to roam but I still pray someday God will bring them back home forever to roam again with the American Indian.

Three Simple Rules

Brian Perry

Three Simple Rules

First Edition: 2022

ISBN: 9781524318178
ISBN eBook: 9781524328290

© of the text:
Brian Perry

© Layout, design and production of this edition: 2022
EBL

Table of Contents

Chapter 1

It was hard to get motivated that morning. Ashley just wanted to stay in bed. The radio said the temperature outside was negative fifteen with a windchill of thirty-five below. She knew she had to get up and get going, but had absolutely no motivation to step out into the frigid morning. She was too comfortable and warm wrapped in her special blanket. Her mother had given her that blanket on her wedding day, and she had kept and cherished it ever since.

Her father had died in an industrial accident when she was only three, and she had no memory of him. Her mother, Sonja, had raised her until she was thirteen. That is when she met Garry. They dated for a while and got married when Ashley was sixteen. He was a great stepfather. Over time, she even felt he was a great father. He took her fishing at the park and taught her to dance and how to stand up for herself. He hunted, fished, enjoyed sports, and helped teach her those. The only two things that she excelled in and enjoyed was the fishing and watching baseball. She could gut a deer and process the meat, but felt they were too pretty to eat. He got her into softball, in which her team got state championship. He would interview and interrogate the boys she would bring home throughout high school.

Her freshman year of college, she met Sarah in one of her classes, and they quickly became friends. After a month or so, Sarah introduced her to her brother, Mark. They hit it off great, just like old friends. They had coffee at the Quad, sodas at dinner on campus, and had even fallen asleep together in the library, before Mark had been taken home for Garry's approval. Even though it was a mere formality, she trusted Garry's opinion, and she loved him as a father. She warned Mark about Garry before getting his approval to date.

As the alarm sounded for the third time, she finally turned it off, wishing she had hit snooze again. She knew the day had to start; people were depending on her. As she got up, she thought a nice hot bath would be the best way to start her day.

As she lay soaking in the tub, relaxing, her phone rang. She knew it was probably Tim calling, making sure she was awake on such a blistery morning. She had prepared for this